Slide Guitar
KNOW THE PLAYERS, PLAY THE MUSIC

Pete Madsen

Slide Guitar

Pete Madsen

A BACKBEAT BOOK
First edition 2005
Published by Backbeat Books
600 Harrison Street
San Francisco, CA 94107, US
www.backbeatbooks.com

An imprint of The Music Player Network CMP Media LLC

Published for Backbeat Books by Outline Press Ltd,
2A Union Court, 20-22 Union Road, London SW4 6JP, England
www.backbeatuk.com

ISBN 0-87930-852-4

EDITOR John Morrish
DESIGN Paul Cooper Design

Printed by SNP Excel (China) Company Ltd.

05 06 07 08 09 5 4 3 2 1

CONTENTS

Rory Gallagher (above), a master of blues-flavored rock, was a hard-working performer who never sought stardom. Mississippi Fred McDowell (opposite top) worked as a farmer, playing fish fries and parties at weekends before making his first recordings at age 55. With his fine technique and encyclopedic range of styles, Ry Cooder (opposite below) is an inspiration to today's slide players.

Slide Guitar

STYLES & PLAYERS

STYLES & PLAYERS

IN 1919, a 17-year-old Hawaiian boy named Solomon Ho'opi'i Ka'ai stowed away on an ocean liner bound for the United States. His dream was to make music for a living. He arrived in San Francisco and quickly moved to Los Angeles, where he formed a trio with Glenwood Leslie and Lani McIntyre. Little did Sol Hoopii know that the music he would end up recording in the years 1927-38, songs like 'Hula Blues,' 'Farewell Blues,' and 'Hawaiian March,' would influence a legion of guitar players from rural Mississippi, who in turn would influence another legion of guitarists decades later from across the Atlantic ocean. Hoopii did not invent slide guitar, but the popularity of these early Hawaiian 'slack key' guitar recordings would go on to be heard around the nation. The sound of a hard comb or steel bar being dragged across the strings had a haunting timbre that would creep into the souls of people around the world.

From its primitive beginnings to its maturity in the age of electric rock'n'roll, slide guitar has given the guitarist a voice that extends the emotional range of the instrument. The slide allowed guitarists to find the notes between notes; the place between the frets where the slippery quality of human emotion runs. The slide can make the strings growl or whimper; it can be bold and menacing or quiet and sympathetic. The slide can keep a run going, circling the perimeters of chord changes; or it could stop it dead in its tracks and give the listener something to ponder.

Slide playing is personal; no two slide players sound alike. How can this be when everybody plays the same Robert Johnson riff? But so many variables, from heart to mind to physical approach, dictate how one plays that riff. I could play it and the odds are when you play it back to me it will sound different. It's because we all hear something different in those notes between the notes, that space where the slide meets the string and is expressed by the individual in an infinite number of ways. Slide playing is elusive and alludes to something we can never fully capture in words.

So where did it come from, and who were the pioneers of slide?

Early Hawaiian slide and resonator guitar

IT IS HARD TO PINPOINT the origin of slide guitar. It really has several origins, including roots in Hawaii and West Africa. In Hawaii, during the 1800s, Portuguese and Mexican sailors introduced guitars to the native population. The Hawaiians adapted the guitar to their own style of music. They tuned the guitar to open chords, often by tuning the guitar 'down' or 'slackening' the strings. A knife blade, comb, or bone would be dragged across the strings to produce a sustained glissando.

Joseph Kekeku is credited with inventing the Hawaiian style in the early 1880s. His recordings, along with those of later players such as Hoopii, Frank Ferera and Jim and Bob (The Genial Hawaiians), were well received and popular during the 1920s and early 1930s. It is said that before 1930 every Chinese restaurant, beer garden, and hotel had its own Hawaiian band.

Hoopii was one of the first guitarists to popularize the steel guitar. The sound of the steel guitar, chillingly evocative, is what many people associate with the sound of early slide playing. Manufactured by the Dopyera brothers, National steel guitars were first conceived as a way for guitarists to compete in volume with a jazz band. The wood guitars of the era were not electrified and could hardly create the same volume as brass or percussion instruments. The National guitars were made of brass or steel, with an innovative 'resonator' design that amplified the sound of the strings by the use of a 'biscuit' (single cone) or 'T-bar' (Tricone) that transferred the vibration of the strings to something resembling a speaker cone(s). These guitars were not only loud; when applying an open tuning and slide techniques to them they produced an even more haunting and evocative sound than that of ordinary wood guitars. That sound is most often associated with rural blues and such players as Charlie Patton, Son House, and Tampa Red.

The National guitars (and later Dobro guitars: a falling out between business partners led the Dopyera brothers to split off from National and form this new company) came in round and square neck versions. The square neck guitars were meant to be played on the lap, with the strings set far above the neck. These guitars were impossible to fret by conventional standards and were meant to be played strictly with a steel bar slid across the strings. To compensate for their inability to fret the guitar with their hands, square-neck players evolved several different tunings and techniques to allow them to play chords and melodies beyond major and minor triads. The square neck guitars evolved into what country players use today: the pedal steel guitar. The pedal steel is a form of lap-style guitar with as many as three separate necks.

The round neck Nationals, on the other hand, were meant to be played like a conventional guitar and thus became popular with many blues musicians. Tampa Red was the first blues artist to record with a National. His music was fairly sophisticated for a bluesman and his playing usually accompanied an orchestra or band. In contrast to Red were Son House, Charlie Patton and Bukka White, who played hard driving, primitive yet extremely evocative material that seemed to come from the earth itself.

Sol Hoopii

Solomon Ho'opi'I Ka'ai'ai was born in 1902 in Honolulu, Hawaii, the youngest of 21 children. At an early age he began playing ukulele and soon brought the guitar and Hawaiian guitar into his instrumental repertoire. Hoopii's stowaway trip almost ended in disaster when he and his two companions were discovered on the boat, with the captain of the ship stymied because he couldn't kick the men off in the middle of the Pacific. The Hawaiian trio's answer was to charm the passengers with their music. The passengers were so elated they all pitched in to pay the trio's fare – or so the story goes.

Hoopii is considered the most influential Hawaiian guitarist of the 20th century. He also had considerable influence on western swing and country pedal steel guitar, and, in as much as he was responsible for popularizing the National guitar, was also an influence on blues artists of the day. (It was reciprocal, however; Hoopii also borrowed a lot from blues players.) When he performed songs like 'Hula Blues,' it was hard to deny the influence.

> **"Hoopii is considered the most influential Hawaiian guitarist of the 20th century."**

His group, The Sol Hoopii Novelty Trio, gained a certain amount of fame during the late 1920s as a performing and recording group. Their records were not only a hit nationally, but became international best-sellers. He was so popular at one point that he appeared in several Hollywood movies, including *Waikiki Wedding*, *Song of the Islands*, and a few Charlie Chan movies. His playing also adorns the soundtrack to a Betty Boop cartoon, *Betty's Bamboo Isle*.

Hoopii's earliest recording was in 1925 with The Waikiki Hawaiian Trio. His playing consisted mainly of rapid-fire single-string runs on a Lyon and Healy flat-top guitar. As his playing developed, he created even more complex chordal and melodic ideas. In 1935 he switched to lap steel guitar, using innovative tunings such as C# minor: B, D, E, G#, C#, E (low to high). The new tunings that he discovered opened up chordal and melodic possibilities that the standard Hawaiian tunings (open A or G) did not possess.

GUITAR: National tricone.

SONGS: 'Hula Blues,' 'Farewell Blues.'

The blues slide tradition

FOR CENTURIES, MUSICIANS in West Africa were using a bow-like instrument strung over a gourd and playing it over their stomachs. This instrument is still used in Africa today and is played by using an object, such as a bone, placed over the string and slid to alter the pitch. African slaves brought to America had very few possessions but were able to adapt and make versions of this instrument by nailing a piece of bailing wire to the floor or wall of a hut and sliding something, once again a bone or metal object, along the string. The early American version of this instrument was called a 'jitterbug.' There is also a version of this instrument that still exists today called the 'diddley bow.' Now you know where Bo Diddley got his name.

The Delta blues men were most likely aware of the recordings of the early Hawaiian players, but adapted their playing to their own style. For instance, instead of holding the guitar on their laps and playing a square neck guitar like the Hawaiian players, the blues players played the guitar in its standard position and used a conventional round neck guitar (except for the bluesman Black Ace, who played the square-neck variety of National guitar). Also, the Hawaiian players favored tunings such as open A (EAEAC#E, low to high), E7 (EBG#DBE), or C# minor (BDEG#C#E). The blues players favored open D (DADF#AD), open E (EBEG#BE), or open G (DGDGBD). While this may seem like a technical point, it is important to note that the relative pitches of the strings would affect how the player approached the instrument and the phrasing of what they played; the general characteristics of the music were bound not only by slide technique but how the player was able to navigate the fret board based on the guitar's tuning.

As the blues tradition evolved, the guitar became more prominent. It was the perfect instrument for the solo performer – infinitely more portable than a piano in rural Mississippi. It also had distinct advantages over the violin or banjo in that it was a better match for the human vocal register. A solo guitarist was welcome at a barn dance, parlor, or front porch jam session, where they would not only sing and play to the delight of the audience but were also expected to provide danceable tunes. Think about how hard it would be today for one person to not only entertain an audience but keep them dancing and you gain a new respect for these early blues guitarists.

As the playing evolved so did the slide. Originally knife blades and combs were used. It was the bluesmen who started to use tubes of metal, brass or glass – the best object being a broken or cut off top of a wine bottle. This allowed the player to put the slide over one finger and leave the others available for fretting chords and notes.

The early blues tradition
The music of the early bluesmen was not intended for a large audience, so it seems to have a deeply personal and resonant tone. As one can imagine, the rural south at the turn of the

BLUES MUSIC WAS A FOLK TRADITION, PASSED DOWN BY WORD OF MOUTH OR ONE-TO-ONE TEACHING. THE EARLY RECORDINGS OF BLIND BLAKE (LEFT) AND ROBERT JOHNSON (BELOW) SHOW WHAT INNOVATIVE AND GREAT PLAYERS THEY WERE.

20th century was wide open; there was lots of space and distances were not easily traveled. Nor was there much money to be made as a musician. Most of the musicians, including Robert Johnson and Mississippi John Hurt (opposite page), made their livings as farmers. In order to make money playing music, they would often have to travel as far as northern cities such as Chicago, as Johnson sometimes did.

There was also a tradition of 'borrowing.' Players would use each other's licks and tricks, yet the ones we remember always gave the music their own personal stamp. The blues tradition was a folk tradition: passed down by word of mouth or one-to-one teaching. It was and is not well served by modern recording techniques and studio trickery. We are fortunate that we have the early recordings of Johnson, Skip James, Bill Broonzy, Blind Willie McTell, Tampa Red, Blind Blake, Son House, Charlie Patton, and Blind Lemon Jefferson as a reminder of how truly innovative and great these players were.

Where blues comes from

Today the source of inspiration for most slide guitarists can be traced back to the blues artists of the early 20th century. To understand what the slide and blues evoke, it is worth examining the cultural circumstances in which the blues arose.

In 1910, 80 per cent of all black people in the South lived in rural areas, and the explosion of black music and creativity reflected this demographic. To say that life was hard for southern blacks would be a gross understatement. Only a few decades on from the Civil War, the institutionalized racism that defined the south was still in full force. With separate facilities for blacks and whites, Jim Crow laws, weekly lynchings, and shifting seasonal employment, life for Southern blacks was bleak but filled with promises of freedom and opportunity that were never delivered.

Many blacks were 'sharecroppers' and were little better off as free men than they were under slavery. Under the state laws of the 1890s, black farmhands were virtually prevented

MISSISSIPPI JOHN HURT

from leaving the land. If they were allowed to leave it was usually under the strict law of unscrupulous landowners. A one-time black sharecropper, writing of his experience, said, "Like other Negro sharecroppers, we were always moving, always in hope of finding a landlord who would not take advantage of us. But we hardly ever succeeded in bettering our position."

Jim Crow laws, ordering segregation in public places, spread throughout the area from 1890 to 1910, requiring separate accommodation for blacks and whites on railroads and other public areas. White supremacy and hatred of blacks increased as competition for jobs replaced the paternalism of slavery. The political and economic machinery favored whites and the frustrations of the freed slaves grew.

The church became the outlet for the blacks' frustrations; it was at this time that blues and gospel music began to evolve on parallel lines. Many early bluesmen were also preachers, eg, Reverend Gary Davis (left) and Son House. The church, however, often proved inadequate as an outlet, especially for young blacks, who were forced to move in order to find work.

It was both hard to leave and hard to stay for blacks in the South. Naturally, they had family ties and close relationships and these proved to be the only stabilizing factor in their lives. Yet, the world as it was defined for them was narrow and limiting, bound by fear and frustration. Often the hope of a better life was sought in the North, in cities like Chicago. (In Robert Johnson's song, 'Sweet Home Chicago' he talks of "going to California, sweet home Chicago." The confusion here is that Chicago is not in the state of California. California was a synonym for 'the land of milk and honey.' Thus, sweet home Chicago represented the land where a blues man could fulfill his dreams.)

> ❝ **The blues is an escape for people who feel frustrations and fears but can't express them.** ❞

In the evolution of the music of the blues we can hear the culmination of these fears, frustrations, joys, sorrows, and longings. The bluesman Henry Townsend says, explaining the relevance of the blues to his audience, "People in general they takes the song as an explanation for themselves – they believe this song is expressing their feelings instead of the one that's singin' it."

The blues becomes an escape for the people who are feeling frustrations and fears but are unable to express them. Perhaps this describes why blues is appreciated on a universal level, why not only blacks but people from other cultural backgrounds appreciate the blues, relating to the musical and emotional components in this music of frustration and longing. Regardless of race, nation, or sex, the blues connects people with the emotional urgency of hopes and desires that can never be fully met.

These were the conditions under which the blues tradition arose. But why don't the songs, in their lyrics, speak of the oppression? The music rarely discussed the roots of oppression, because to have done so would have opened the door to even more lynchings

and hardship. Instead, the lyrical content of blues favored a general rather than specific dissatisfaction with life. It was, for instance, permissible to discuss the dissatisfactions in male-female relationships.

There were also stories of folk heroes such as John Henry and Stagolee. These stories were usually warnings of what might happen to the 'bad man,' or what might happen if you stepped out of line. The lawman was always there to keep you in line. The lyrics were really a thinly-veiled metaphor for the oppression blacks felt.

The popularity of blues in the Mississippi Delta was particularly strong. The area's huge plantations were worked by sharecroppers. Blacks were also able to find work in a number of other occupations: building levees to hold back the waters of the 'Mighty' Mississippi, cutting timber, and building the railroads that would carry the crops to market. Where the work was hard – in mining towns, tobacco plantations, work camps, and prisons – the blues thrived in gambling dens, saloons, and brothels as well as in 'legitimate' house parties, fish fries, barbecue stands, and railway stations.

Around 1905, bandleader W.C. Handy was dozing at a train station in Tutwiler, Mississippi, when he had his first encounter with the blues. A young man approached him playing guitar and using a knife as a slide. Handy wrote about his encounter, "His clothes were rags; his feet peeped out of shoes. His face had on it some of the sadness of the ages… The singer repeated the line three times, accompanying himself on the guitar with the weirdest music I had ever heard. The tune stayed in my mind." For bandleaders like Handy and the general populace, the music of the era was saturated with novelty tunes and peppy numbers that would be forgotten in a week's time, like any number of Britney Spears songs. The music this young ragged man was playing "stayed" with Handy. Even though it was "weird" there was a quality that haunted him.

The lyrical qualities of blues could range from poetic to frank discussions of sex, to wails, moans, and humming. The vocal was not merely an expression of words with musical notes attached. The vocal was delivered in the manner that was truthful to the expression of the artist. The non-lyrical quality of many of these performances is also wrapped up in the anguish that was the black experience. The guitar playing reflected this sentiment: it was a mournful wailing. It could be hard and visceral, or soft and playful. The slide guitarist could bring these sentiments to the fore with his voice, his guitar and his slide.

The music of the blues

But blues did not just show up on the doorstep one day; nor was it really 'discovered' by explorers like Handy. To say that any form of music is created in a vacuum would be wrong. This is especially true of rural American music, which was passed on from group to group and evolved through the contributions of both blacks and whites, as well as other races and cultures. In particular, blacks had adopted Anglo-American folk-ballad traditions and adapted them to their own musical traditions. Characters such as John Henry, a spike driver on a railroad who "died with a hammer in his hand," were created out of this folk-ballad tradition. Other folk characters, such as Stagolee, were often 'bad men' who suffered for their transgressions: a black southern version of a morality play.

The white folk ballads were sung unaccompanied, but the black ballads incorporated the guitar, banjo, harmonica, and other instruments. Somewhere along the line the 'blue note' became a part of the blues vernacular. In musical terms the blue note is represented by a dynamic tension between two notes (most often the major and minor third, but sometimes including other notes of pentatonic and seven-note western scales, as well). The blues player would bend or slide back and forth between the two notes, sometimes resolving the tension and sometimes not. The blue note(s) has become as synonymous with the blues as the 12-bar structure.

(The 12-bar structure actually evolved later on, with electric and ensemble blues. The solo artists of the earlier 20th century had a little more freedom in their interpretation of rhythmic structures. Sometimes they used 13 bars or 14, sometimes partial bars were included, and time signature shifts often occurred; going from 6/8 to

THE SINGERS MA RAINEY (TOP LEFT, WITH HER GEORGIA JAZZ BAND) AND BESSIE SMITH (LEFT) WERE AMONG THE FIRST BLUES ARTISTS WHOSE PERFORMANCES WERE RECORDED.

4/4 and then maybe to 12/4 for a while. It was all up to the individual to express the song in whatever rhythmic, melodic or non-melodic way they felt.)

Slide guitar helped emphasize the blue note by allowing the player to achieve that 'slippery' quality – that elusiveness that is integral to the blues. The blues, thought by many to be a technically limiting genre, has some deep nuances that are often difficult to explain. Musical phrasings are often individual interpretations: how different artists interpret the blue note(s) could be a subject for a long essay.

In the beginning no one considered himself strictly a blues musician. Indeed, the genre at this point had hardly been defined. Most of the players drew upon spirituals, ragtime tunes and other popular tunes of the day to perform in public. But the popularity of the music grew and bandleaders like W.C. Handy started to incorporate blues into their bands' sets. In the 1920s the phonograph replaced sheet music as the best way to promote the blues. This was a blessing and a curse in that now a larger audience was being exposed to the music via records. Blues performers were beginning to make names for themselves. But their recordings were marketed as 'race' records and sold strictly to black audiences. Many of these records went virtually unnoticed until the advent of a more open and democratic radio system in the 1950s.

The first blues singers to record, in the early 1920s, were based in New York. They included Ma Rainey and Bessie Smith and were backed by the top jazz musicians of the day, including Louis Armstrong, King Oliver and Jelly Roll Morton.

In 1925 recording techniques improved and portability became a factor in transporting the equipment to the rural south. Electricity and the microphone were better suited to picking up the rural accents and guitar than the old acoustic horn technique. Record companies started sending people out to capture the sounds of rural America with the new portable recording equipment. These early sessions were held in rented motel rooms, churches and auditoriums.

The rise of the guitar

Many factors led to the rise of the guitar as the featured instrument in blues. First, but not foremost, was the expansion of the railroad. Between 1860 and 1910, railroad construction averaged 4,000 miles per year. In the South the main construction linking it with the rest of the nation occurred between 1893 and 1904. With the railroad network firmly in place, postal delivery increased and thus was born the Sears and Roebuck catalog.

Ordering through a catalog, rural dwellers had access to goods that they had previously only dreamed of. Initially, the catalog didn't advertise musical instruments, but by 1905 more than 60 pages were dedicated to guitars, ukuleles, saxophones, trumpets, banjos, and violins. Blacks, most likely, were not the initial purchasers of these instruments. In the 1897 catalog, guitars ranged in price from $3.25-$27.00, more than most blacks of the time could afford. As the novelty of the original purchase wore off, however, and the purchaser realized that playing the instrument required some work, the instruments often found their way to pawnshops. Blacks were often the fortunate beneficiaries of bored whites when it came to guitar pawnshop purchases.

Another factor in the rise of the guitar among bluesmen was the decline of the banjo. The banjo had been the main instrument of minstrel shows. The parodying of blacks in these shows had become less tolerable to the black community in a time of social change. However, many of the techniques that were used with banjos, such as open tunings, were transferred to the guitar. This was a major attraction for the slide player who used the open tunings to great advantage. Able to accompany themselves using finger-picking techniques like banjo players, the more skilled players could keep separate bass and melody lines going at the same time. Also the timbre of the guitar was better suited to the soloist's vocal register: the banjo having a raspier sound, and the guitar a mellower and more lyrical quality.

A host of blues pioneers sprang forth in this era of expansion. Many of the players had a style that could be associated with a particular area of the South. There was the Texas sound, the Delta sound and the Piedmont sound, to name a few. None had quite the impact of the early Delta players, who pioneered a style of playing that drifted northward to Chicago where it evolved into the electric blues we know today.

> **"The early Delta players pioneered a style that became the electric blues we know today."**

The evolution of the guitar

Guitars prior to the 1930s were small. As the demand for bass increased, the instrument became bigger. The Dreadnought – named after a famous British battleship – was introduced by Martin in 1931. This became the favored instrument of country and bluegrass pickers: with its boomy sound, guitarists could create a big sound with the emphasis on the bottom. Blues players, however, concentrated on licks and melodies and preferred the smaller-bodied Gibsons. Also, for financial reasons, blues artists favored the less expensive Stellas and Regals of the day.

Until 1930, guitar necks joined the body at the 12th fret. After 1930 it became fashionable to make guitars with necks that joined at the 14th fret, giving players access to higher notes. A lot of slide playing is centered around the 12th fret (especially in open tunings). Having access to higher frets could give the music that extra little nudge of wildness that would open the door to the slide-playing histrionics of rock players

Resophonic Guitars

In 1927 when resophonic guitars first appeared on the market they were valued for their volume. Today, they are valued for their tone. In a normal wood guitar the vibration of the strings sets the whole top of the guitar in motion; with a resonator guitar the string vibration passes through the cone, a structure looking a little like a pie plate. Just like a loudspeaker, the cone of the resonator guitar amplifies the sound. Being made of metal, it gives the sound a metallic twang. In order for the cone to amplify most effectively, resophonic guitars are usually strung with medium- to heavy-gauged strings and are played with fingerpicks.

These guitars seemed to have been designed with slide players in mind – although they weren't. There are not many sounds as distinctive as a slide being used on a resonator guitar. It spells rural blues. Particularly good for slide playing is the National resonator guitar.

National was the company that introduced the resonator concept. Originally designed for the guitarist competing with saxophones, trumpets, drums, and other instruments in an orchestra, it fell out of favor when electric guitars were introduced. However, Hawaiian and blues players seemed to capture the essence of the instrument with their slide techniques.

The first design was the popular Tricone, comprised of three small resonators linked by a T-bar. The Tricone was by far the most sophisticated of the resonator instruments. These first instruments were made of brass with a nickel plating. They often had very ornate engravings: palm trees and Hawaiian Island themes predominated. In order to provide more economical versions of the resonator guitar the company introduced the single cone, Style O, and later the modestly priced Duolian. These later and more economical versions substituted steel for brass and had a harsher tone that was ideal for the tough sounds coming from artists such as Son House.

A few years after the first Nationals made their way to the market a split in the company led the Dopyera brothers (the original designers) to leave and start their own company: Dobro. Because of patent restrictions, the Dopyeras were forced to design a new resonator style and hence the Dobro was born. In a dobro the cone is connected to the bridge indirectly, via a strutwork apparatus called a 'spider,' rather than the National T-bar and 'biscuit' bridges.

The different designs of cone lend different tonal qualities to Dobros and Nationals. Dobros tend to have a slightly 'nasal' quality. In Dobros the resonator is normally resting in a wood-topped guitar – in Nationals it is usually resting inside a metal guitar, although both companies made wood and metal models. Dobros tend to be favored by country and bluegrass musicians, and Nationals tend to be preferred by blues musicians.

In the 1980s the National Guitar Company returned to making high-quality resonator instruments. The earlier models from the late 1920s and 1930s are still highly sought after, however, the new models are of a superior quality and sit high above most of the other resonator guitars on the market today.

Charlie Patton

Not enough can be said about the influence of Charlie Patton (top right), who was born in 1891 near Bolton in southern Mississippi. Some call Patton the original founder of the Delta blues – he was one of Robert Johnson's 'mentors.' Son House, Howlin' Wolf, Muddy Waters, Elmore James, and John Lee Hooker can all trace their styles back to Patton.

Patton lived on Will Dockery's plantation between Drew and Boyle in rural Mississippi. He began to have some success as a musician as early as 1910 but it wasn't until the late 1920s that he became recognized as 'the man.' Between 1929 and 1930 Patton recorded 42 issued sides, more than any other blues artist had turned out in one year. Patton's vocal style was a rich baritone; a voice that was both raw and visceral. His playing style was also raw

and visceral; a great performer, Patton sometimes played the guitar behind his back or on his knees. He had a reputation as a drunk and as a womanizer (he reportedly had eight wives), and his hard living ended his life prematurely in 1934 at the age of 42.

He was a regional success and inspired many of the guitarists of the day, not only with his guitar playing and acrobatic performance style, but with his nice clothes, cars, fancy guitars, and female admirers.

He was a small, slight man with wavy hair who had inherited his mother's facial features: mixed Indian, black and white. His parents provided a stable atmosphere on their farm in Mississippi, hoping that Charlie would maintain their position in the community. Charlie, however, wanted to play guitar and have fun. When the family moved to the Dockery plantation, Patton started to learn guitar from a man named Henry Sloan.

In 1929 Patton met Henry Spier, a white music-store owner (and talent scout) who sent him north to record for the Paramount Blues label. His recordings represented him at his best and it was said that he was a much better singer on record than he was in live performance. However, the recordings didn't change his life much; he still had to perform every night to make a living. He continued to play for audiences all over the South, not just blacks but whites as well.

He developed a couple of different slide techniques. Using both the knife blade and bottleneck techniques, Patton was able to get various effects from the guitar, creating high pitches by playing far up the fretboard; as well, he was able to use the sustaining quality of the slide for slow drag tunes, such as 'Banty Rooster.' In 'Mississippi Boweavil Blues' and 'Spoonful Blues' one can hear Patton's percussive alternating bass combined with flawless bottleneck technique.

SONGS: 'Spoonful Blues,' 'Mississippi Boweavil Blues.'
GUITAR: Early Gibson or Stella.

Son House

One of Patton's protégés was Son House. Son House (1902-1988) was not as well known as some of his peers, such as Robert Johnson and Charlie Patton, but he was one of the most powerful of the group – and he outlived them by a good 50 years. His playing was primitive, not flashy, and his vocal delivery was nothing if not impassioned. In his slide playing one could hear personal demons being fought, like the licking of flames at the boots of a mortal sinner.

Born near Lyon, Mississippi, House chopped cotton as a teenager while developing a passion for the Baptist church. At an early age he became a preacher, but had a falling out with the church after having an affair with a woman ten years his senior.

In 1926 he began playing guitar, learning from an obscure local musician named James

SON HOUSE

McCoy. But in 1928, at a house party near Lyon, House shot and killed a man. He was sentenced to work at Parchman Farm, a State penitentiary that also housed Bukka White and that became notorious for its ill-treatment of its prisoners. A judge reexamined the case and House was released after 18 months. House was advised to leave the area and so he picked up and moved to the Clarksdale vicinity, where he struck up a friendship with Charlie Patton.

In 1930 House traveled with Patton to Grafton, Wisconsin, where he recorded his first sides. These early recordings established him as a powerful voice in the world of the blues. However, they did not lead to commercial success. There were no further recordings until Alan Lomax recorded him for the Library of Congress in 1941, and then again no recordings until the folk revival of the 1960s.

In the 1960s he could be seen at many festivals, playing his National resonator guitar and stomping his feet like a wild man. It was partly the rediscovery of House and his peers by a new white audience that helped propel a renewed interest in the blues. In his playing there was as much percussive attack – popping the strings, vocal groans – as there was melody. Often melody seemed to be sacrificed for the outpouring of emotion that came out in House's performances. He alternated his single note slide runs with descending bass lines. House truly seemed like a man haunted by demons. When he played slide it was like shards of glass on hard pavement, not always a pleasing sound, but a raw and truthful one.

SONG: 'Empire State Blues.'

GUITAR: National Triolian, Duolian, or Style O.

Robert Johnson

The myth of Robert Johnson, the most influential of the early blues men, says that he sold his soul to the devil at the crossroads for his amazing guitar talent. He is credited with giving birth to rock'n'roll, and has influenced artists such as The Rolling Stones, Led Zeppelin, Eric Clapton and many others. Clapton plays tribute to Johnson on his 2004 recording, *Me and Mr. Johnson*, showcasing several songs from Johnson's repertoire. Today, if people are not familiar with who Johnson was, they certainly know his songs – 'Dust My Broom,' 'Sweet Home Chicago,' 'Walkin' Blues' – which have been repeatedly recorded by artists over the decades.

Robert Johnson was born May 8th, 1911, in Hazlehurst, Mississippi, to Julia Dodds and Noah Johnson. His ten siblings were fathered by another man, Charles Dodds. Apparently, Dodds was a furniture maker and landowner and financially solvent until a falling out with some local landowners. As the story goes, Dodds was being sought by a lynch mob and made his escape to Memphis by dressing like a woman.

Eventually, Julia Dodds was forced off her land for non-payment of taxes and spent the next eight years trying to reunite her children with their father, Charles. Robert was considered illegitimate and while he was eventually accepted by Charles Dodds, Dodds never accepted Julia back. Robert is said to have adopted the name of Johnson in his teens when he learned who his real father was. Perhaps some of the mystery revolving around Robert Johnson stems from the various monikers he adopted at different points in his life. He went by the names of Robert Spencer, R.L. Spencer, and sometimes Robert Dodds.

In 1914 Johnson went to live in Memphis with his adopted father and a family that included Dodds' children, mistress and their two children. It was here that Robert began to learn guitar from his brother, Charles Leroy.

Son House, speaking about Robert Johnson, says: "We'd play for Saturday night balls, and there would be this little boy hanging around. He blew a harmonica and he was pretty good with that, but he wanted to play guitar." The myth that Johnson sold his soul to the devil stems from this period. At the time that House was speaking of, Johnson couldn't play the guitar at all. When House next saw Johnson a few months later, guitar strung over his back, he was awed by Johnson's playing. It was thought that the boy had to have sold his soul to devil in order to get that good that quickly.

Not only had Johnson become proficient on the instrument, he was a gifted entertainer who established an immediate rapport with his audience. Wherever he went he was remembered for his warmth. His repertoire included not just the blues sides we have today, but whatever his audience wanted to hear: Bing Crosby tunes, country tunes, hillbilly tunes, Duke Ellington songs. His traveling companion, Johnny Shines, claims that Robert had an ability to play anything. He would hear it once and play it right back.

By the middle 1930s Robert was well known throughout the Delta areas and had followings in southern Mississippi and eastern Tennessee. He had wanted to make records for some years, as his mentors Willie Brown, Son House, and Charlie Patton had done. In 1936 Johnson got his chance to record, indirectly, through the same man who had recorded Son House, Patton, and Skip James. H.C. Spier was a white man working for ARC records and had recorded 200 sides in Jackson and Hattiesberg. Only 40 had been issued, however, so he passed Johnson's name on to Ernie Oertle, a talent scout and salesman for ARC in the mid-South. In November they traveled to San Antonio, TX. He recorded 16 sides in three days, including 'I Believe I'll Dust My Broom,' and 'Kind Hearted Woman.'

In all, Johnson recorded 29 sides between 1936 and 1938, all of which have been reissued numerous times. He died in 1938 from poisoning by a jealous husband; he was 27 years old. Of his slide playing, probably his most memorable track is 'Come On In My Kitchen.' Johnson blended rhythm, lead, riffs, and vocals in a way that was entirely his own. He would play a slide line and moan along with it; he would then break into a shuffle rhythm and complement that with single-note lead lines.

All we have left to remember Johnson are those 29 sides and one photo (see page 12) in which he is wearing a fancy suit and holding a nice Gibson guitar (probably borrowed). His blues have a brooding sense of torment and despair. The mystery of what tormented Johnson is almost as provocative as his actual playing. In Peter Guralnick's book, *Searching for Robert Johnson*, it is easy to understand the appeal: "What could be more appropriate to our sense of romantic mystery than an emotionally disturbed poet scarcely able to contain

> **"Johnson was a gifted entertainer who established an immediate rapport with his audience and was remembered for his warmth."**

his 'brooding sense of torment and despair'? ... So Robert Johnson became the personification of the existential blues singer, unencumbered by corporeality or history, a fiercely incandescent spirit who had escaped the bonds of tradition by the sheer thrust of genius."

For all the emotional impact of the recordings of Robert Johnson left us, there is also this: he played some amazing guitar. His slide playing is of the highest caliber: he would use single-line runs, and yet there was the multi-string triplet attack that powered tunes like 'Dust My Broom.' 'Come On In My Kitchen' has one of most recognizable and eloquent single-string opening phrases ever recorded. That opening phrase combined with the hummed part are at once suggestive, sad and beautiful; pleading and at the same time demanding.

Even if you are not a Robert Johnson fan, there is no denying the influence passed down to future generations of blues and slide players.

SONGS: 'Come On In My Kitchen,' 'Dust My Broom.'

GUITAR: Gibson L1.

Tampa Red

Tampa Red or 'The Guitar Wizard' was the first big star from Chicago's blues scene. His real name was Hudson Whittaker. Born in Smithsville, Georgia, he was orphaned at an early age

and moved to Tampa, Florida, to live with his grandparents. The red-headed Tampa worked as a musician and on the vaudeville circuit until he moved to Chicago in the mid-1920s. There he started working with Tom Dorsey and together they invented a new kind of blues called hokum (light and peppy numbers filled with lyrical double-entendres).

Tampa played with the house band at Bluebird Records, helping to establish the 'Bluebird Beat,' which was the sound coming out of the Chicago record label at the time. He was also very helpful to others in the blues scene. He opened his house to other artists in need, fans, and foreign visitors.

Tampa continued to record into the early 1950s, but rock'n'roll was taking over most of the business. He retired in 1953, having recorded more than 320 sides. In 1955, his wife Frances died. Tampa struggled with this and began to drink heavily. In 1960, he cut two more albums for the Prestige-Bluesville label and completely retired. He died in a nursing home on March 19th, 1981, the same year he was inducted into the Blues Foundation's Hall of Fame.

Tampa Red was a huge influence on bottleneck players of the era. He often played with a band or

accompanist, which allowed him to stretch out and play some complicated single-note slide runs. He also helped popularize National resonator guitars with the blues crowd. He was usually seen playing a National Tricone guitar, an instrument with a more sophisticated sound than its brother, the single resonator (Style O and Duolian), played by Son House. The Tricone seemed to sustain better than the Style O, which had a more immediate attack but a faster decay. Both guitars work well for slide and it is merely a matter of personal taste, although, if you like your blues tone more guttural than complex, I would recommend the single-cone guitars.

SONG: 'Denver Blues.'

GUITAR: National Tricone.

Mississippi Fred McDowell

Born in Rossville, Tennessee, in 1904, Fred McDowell (opposite) eventually settled in Mississippi in 1940. In his younger days, McDowell played for tips on the streets of Memphis, but decided that life on the road wasn't for him and became a farmer. During the week he tended the farm and on the weekends he played house parties and fish fries.

He did not record until 1959, when folklorist Alan Lomax found him and recorded him for the American Folk Music series on Atlantic Records. In 1964, Chris Strachwitz of Arhoolie records hunted down McDowell and recorded a two-volume series which helped propel him into the radar of the folk revivalists.

During this period, McDowell performed at coffee houses and the famous Newport Folk Festival. The Rolling Stones invited him to Europe to play. The Stones reportedly bought McDowell a silver lamé suit that he wore back home and was eventually buried in.

He first learned guitar from an uncle who used a hollow bone for a slide. McDowell was by all accounts a gracious man who freely shared his knowledge of blues and the guitar. He even set up a foundation before he died, using money from his record sales to buy instruments for underprivileged children in northern Mississippi.

SONG: 'Goin' Down to the River.'

GUITAR: Kay acoustic.

Blind Boy Fuller

Some say that Blind Boy Fuller (also known as Fulton Allen) was to the Piedmont blues what Robert Johnson was to the Delta blues. The Piedmont is the area of the south-east United States bordered by the coast and the mountain foothills. He was one of the best selling blues artists of the 1930s, and his songs were learned and covered by many of the East Coast bluesmen who followed. Perhaps he is not as well known as Johnson because Piedmont blues, with its emphasis on ragtime, had less of an influence on the Chicago blues (and rock'n'roll) than the Delta musicians. The hard-driving sounds of the Delta blues lent them a sophistication and flair that the more rural-sounding Piedmont blues lacked.

Fuller was born in 1907 or thereabouts in Wadesboro, North Carolina, south-east of Charlotte. He was one of the few members of his family who took an interest in music, and even he didn't begin to take it seriously until his early twenties. He married a woman named Cora, who became his wife at the tender age of 14. Shortly after their marriage, Fuller began having trouble with his eyesight and became increasing dependent on Cora for help. It was also about this time that he became more interested in music – blindness and being black severely limiting his employment options. Under the tutelage of The Reverend Gary Davis, Fuller gained first competence and then mastery of his chosen instrument, the guitar.

He was earning a decent living busking on the streets of Durham, NC, when he was noticed by J.B. Long, a white man who managed the United Dollar Store. Long had been drumming up country and gospel talent for the American Record Company, and in 1935 he convinced them to record Fuller. The sessions took place in New York with Gary Davis and Richard Trice brought on board. The recordings went so well that Fuller was asked back as a solo artist in April of 1936. Later collaborations included a stint with harmonica legend Sonny Terry.

In 1938 Fuller was diagnosed with arrested syphilis. His health continued to falter and he died on February 13th, 1941.

SONG: 'Homesick And Lonesome Blues.'

GUITAR: National 12- and 14-fret Duolians.

Robert Nighthawk

Robert Nighthawk was a drifter. He was born Robert McCullum on November 30th, 1909, in Helena, Arkansas. His travels brought him into contact with Charlie Patton, Robert Johnson, John Lee Hooker, Muddy Waters, Elmore James and B.B. King. In the mid 1930s he left the Deep South, where he was reported to have shot a man, for St. Louis. In the late 1930s he returned to Chicago to record 'Prowling Night-Hawk,' one of his most popular records. Thus was Robert 'Nighthawk' created.

His slide playing is smooth, some would say 'liquid.' His single-string melodies complemented his dark and melancholy-tinted voice.

GUITAR: Gibson electric.

Black Ace

One of the few blues players to use a National Tricone square-neck played on his lap, Black Ace seems to have represented a crossover between blues and Hawaiian guitar. His playing is a bit more sophisticated than Robert Johnson's or Son House's, but he never acquired the same fame as those two. However, he is an important figure in the history of slide guitar.

In the late 1930s, a Texan by the name of Babe Karo Lemon Turner released a single called, 'Black Ace Blues.' A local radio station picked up on the name and it soon became the moniker by which the artist would be known. He disappeared until Chris Strachwitz came to his home in Fort Worth, Texas, in 1960 and recorded him for Arhoolie Records. Along with the earlier recordings from the 1930s, these are the only recordings that exist from Black Ace. Partly because of his lack of a prolific recording career and partly because his playing is not associated with any regional style (eg, Piedmont, Chicago), Ace is a bit of an obscurity. However, in his playing one can hear the blend of a gracious melodic sense, more associated with Hawaiian music, and a blues rhythmic structure.

SONG: 'Black Ace Blues.'

GUITAR: National Tricone.

The blues moves north

CHICAGO

In the 1940s, as blacks left the South for work in the factories up north, the blues also left. Chicago became the cultural center for blues and was the city that launched the careers of artists such as Muddy Waters, Big Bill Broonzy, Tampa Red, and others looking for recording opportunities. When the music moved to this new urban location it began to transform from its rural roots to a more modern sound.

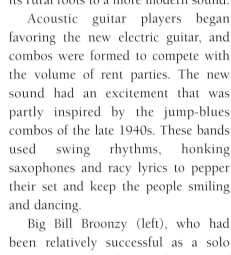

Acoustic guitar players began favoring the new electric guitar, and combos were formed to compete with the volume of rent parties. The new sound had an excitement that was partly inspired by the jump-blues combos of the late 1940s. These bands used swing rhythms, honking saxophones and racy lyrics to pepper their set and keep the people smiling and dancing.

Big Bill Broonzy (left), who had been relatively successful as a solo artist, incorporated a combination of piano, second guitar, horns and drums into his sound.

Muddy Waters used the electric guitar for great effect, launching angry and aggressive slide runs. Waters had started out as a solo acoustic musician, but when he played electric with a band it transformed the music from its lonely rural southern roots to a lively urban sound that electrified the dance floors and virtually paved the way for rock'n'roll. His recordings inspired many of the British rock legends of the 1960s to learn to play blues and seek out old recordings.

Muddy Waters

McKinley Morganfield was born in 1915, in Rolling Rock, Mississippi. He garnered the name 'Muddy' because he loved to play in the water of nearby Deer Creek. At age seven he fell in love with the harmonica. His family attached 'Waters' to the nickname, and it stuck.

His rich tenor voice, singing slightly behind the beat, and a style of slide playing that emphasized the bass strings – as opposed to most slide players, who played leads runs on the treble strings – produced a distinctive voice in the blues.

He recorded for Alan Lomax, the famous Library of Congress musicologist, in 1941. After hearing the recordings he became convinced of his own commercial viability. He moved to Chicago in 1943 where he found work playing rent parties. He gained commercial success with the 1947 release *I Can't be Satisfied*, which quickly sold out several pressings. He returned to the Deep South and often toured there throughout the 1950s and 1960s with John Lee Hooker. In 1958 he toured England and opened the door for bluesmen from the US to play in the UK.

Muddy Waters (opposite) became a more direct influence on future musicians. He brought the solo rural blues and wedded it to a small ensemble, thus defining Chicago's electric blues sound. When the "hoochie-coochie man" got his "mojo workin'" he was a hard man to beat. Muddy Waters died April 30th, 1983, and is buried in Chicago.

Waters was one of the first to amplify his guitar. In increasingly loud venues it became necessary to bring up the volume; as he did so, the guitar had a tendency to distort. This distortion begins to compress the guitar signal, producing increased sustain. The combination of increased distortion and sustain opened a new world for slide guitarists. The sound evolved and players such as Elmore James, Duane Allman, Rory Gallagher and Rod Price used it to create a new sound palette on which slide guitarists could paint their effervescent landscapes.

> "The combination of distortion and sustain opened up a new world for slide guitarists."

As the sound evolved, the guitar was able to emulate not only the human voice but other instruments as well. Heretofore, the natural decay of the sound was rather quick. But with the sustain of electric guitar, the glissando could travel over the interval of several notes: the guitarist could pick one note, for example, and with the use of the slide land on four or five more notes before even needing to pick again. Like a horn player, who was only limited by the amount of wind he could muster, the guitar player could slide more freely between notes. Certain overtones were created; notes between notes became more useful and interesting.

SONG: 'Hoochie Coochie Man.'
GUITAR: Fender Telecaster.

Elmore James

Along with Muddy Waters, Elmore James is one of the few players represented in this book who bridges the gap between the old Delta blues players and the modern blues and rock'n'roll players. He is classified as a post-war musician, not having made his first recordings until 1951. However, he did quite a lot of playing between 1929-50, having shared the stage with such luminaries as Robert Johnson and Sonny Boy Williamson II.

He was born Elmore Brooks in 1918, in Richland, Mississippi. His family moved up and down Highway 51, going from plantation to plantation in search of work. At the age of ten he was playing a self-made guitar, as well as other 'home-made' instruments such as the

MUDDY WATERS

'diddley bow.' Over the next ten years he refined his playing on the streets, at fish fries, and jook joints.

In 1937, the family moved to Belzoni. James's parents adopted another child, Robert Earl Holsten, and the two young men began to play music together in Belzoni. The same year, at age 19, James married a young woman named Josephine Harris. James, however, seemed restless and the wandering life of the road called.

This was also the year that James (right) met two very important men: Robert Johnson and harmonica player, Alec 'Rice' Miller.

Johnson's bottleneck playing left a deep impression on James and it was a style he would emulate and become famous for. He began to travel more often and met Sonny Boy Williamson, who was beginning to make a name for himself from his short performance on a new show on radio station KFFA, advertising King Biscuit Flour. The radio show would grow in popularity over the years and had the largest audience in the South for blues in the following decades.

In 1943 he was inducted into the US Navy, taking part in the invasion of Guam. By 1945 he was back home in Belzoni, sharing a room with Sonny Boy Williamson. In the early 1940s he began playing electric guitar, using distortion and sustain to create a dense sound.

James's first recording for the Trumpet label was Robert Johnson's 'Dust my Broom,' which went to number nine on the national R&B charts. The following year he relocated to Chicago, where he recorded with numerous record companies, including Modern, Chess, Chief, Fire, Fury, and Enjoy Records. He continued to record and perform throughout the 1950s and 1960s. James died on May 24th, 1963, in Chicago, at the age of 45.

Elmore James brought the sound of the Delta to the modern world. He was employing the techniques of Robert Johnson and Charlie Patton, but with an electric guitar and a backing band. This gave the music an energy that propelled it into the sphere of rock'n'roll. You could also say that James helped the world recognize the connection between blues and Hawaiian music – he even recorded a song called 'Hawaiian Boogie.' He left a legacy of slow blues, boogies, and rave ups that inspired such modern day guitarists as Johnny Winter, Rod Price and Rory Gallagher, to name but a few.

SONG: 'Dust My Broom.'

GUITAR: Kay acoustic.

DETROIT

Detroit also became a center for electric blues, launching the careers of such notables as John Lee Hooker. His 'Boogie Chillen' was an extremely popular post-war blues record and placed him on a level with Waters as one of the most popular blues musicians of the time. 'Boogie Chillen,' a danceable boogie that was dark and spooky, harkened to darker themes in the underbelly of blues. Much of Hooker's influence can be heard in the playing of Billy Gibbons of ZZ Top.

John Lee Hooker

John Lee Hooker (below) was born on August 22nd, 1917, on a sharecropper farm south of Clarksdale, Mississippi. He left home in 1933, living the life of a hobo and not really settling down until he reached Detroit in 1943. He had a series of jobs: including a stint in the Receiving Hospital and jobs at Dodge and Comco Steel. During the evenings and on weekends he would play the bars around Detroit. Hooker credits Elmer Barbee with 'discovering' him and leading him on to his successful career path. His first recordings appeared in 1948, from which was spawned his infamous 'Boogie Chillen.' Another of his signature tunes, 'Boom Boom,' was released in 1962.

Hooker made a brief return to acoustic blues in the 1960s, when young bohemian audiences began to embrace early blues artists such as Hooker, Skip James, and John Hurt.

SKIP JAMES

He was a major influence on British artists like John Mayall and The Yardbirds. His most recognized sound is that of his boogie-laden electric guitar recordings. In 1970, Hooker moved to Oakland, California, and the Bay Area remained his home until he died in 2001.

In his later years, Hooker recorded many collaborations with artists such as B.B. King, Ben Harper, Carlos Santana, Robert Cray, and Jimmie Vaughan.

SONG: 'Boogie Chillen.'

GUITAR: Epiphone ES335.

NEW YORK

Many of the bluesmen who wound up in New York were from Virginia, the Carolinas and Georgia. The blues in that part of the US were ragtime influenced, with lots of finger-picking. Players such as the Reverend Gary Davis, Sonny Terry and Brownie McGee, and Mississippi John Hurt played their rural blues intact and were embraced by folk revivalists such as Pete Seeger and Bob Dylan.

After his release from prison, in 1934, Leadbelly (also known as Huddie Ledbetter), moved to New York and went to work for the Lomax family (chroniclers of American folk music for the Library of Congress), and fell in with Woody Guthrie and Pete Seeger.

The stylistic evolution of the blues ended in the 1960s as the civil rights movement began to take hold. Many of the victories of civil rights ameliorated many of the social factors that had contributed to the rise of the blues as a form of expression. The civil rights movement stressed collective action and had little use for the individualistic stance of the blues artist. At the same time, however, interest in the blues began to increase among whites, especially those involved in the folk revival.

The folk revival

FOLK MUSIC IS A GENERAL TERM for roots music that has been handed down from generation to generation via participation in groups or person to person. The folk music revival of the 1950s and 1960s actively sought out the music of America's past: blues, country, Appalachian. This was music that had been created before the advent of recording technology; it is 'the music of the land.' Many of the people seeking and documenting it were people who weren't actually involved in creating it, namely, young white educated people.

Although much criticism has been aimed at the revivalists, a good argument exists for their promotion of the music: imitating the art of another culture gives that culture acknowledgement and visibility. If it weren't for the revivalists, many of the old blues artists might have been completely forgotten and acoustic slide guitar could have been totally lost:

"The movement values above all else the intimacy of personal expression, created by soloists and small ensembles; though the folk revival sometimes mobilized large crowds, its soul was found in intimate gatherings and informal sing-alongs. The roots music that the revival emulated seems to stand for the same kind of personal interactions." (From 'The Flowering Of The Folk Revival,' by Alan Jabbour, in *American Roots Music*, edited by Robert Santelli, Holly George-Warren, and Jim Brown.)

One path these revivalists took was to try and duplicate not so much the songs of the past, but the sound. They modeled their voices on the hillbilly musicians they loved, but put their own stamp on the music by writing their own lyrics and expanding the structure through jamming and instrumental experimentation. Guitarists recaptured the techniques of the early blues artists and sought out vintage instruments to make the sounds they had heard on early 78s by Robert Johnson, Son House, and Charlie Patton. They sought out vintage instruments such as old Gibsons, Nationals, and Dobros. In 1952 the pioneering work of Harry Smith was revealed in the six LP *Anthology of American Folk Music*, a collection of blues, hillbilly, and other folk music from the 1920s. Even today, this anthology stands out as the primer for anyone wishing to indoctrinate himself in American roots music. The *Anthology* was the working bible of the revivalists.

John Fahey

One of these educated youngsters was a man named John Fahey (below). Fahey, with a background in philosophy at the University of California in Berkeley, was one of a handful of young white men who brought the senior bluesmen out of the woodwork. Son House, Skip James, Gary Davis, and John Hurt were able to enjoy a second artistic life in their old age, thanks in part to men like Fahey.

Fahey absorbed their music like a sponge. In the process he brought influences as eclectic as classical music and Indian ragas. His acoustic instrumentals combine the haunting qualities of early blues with the structural development of classical compositions and a droning quality reminiscent of Indian music. His slide playing reflected the stark quality of players like Charlie Patton and Black Ace.

The eccentric and idiosyncratic Fahey was raised in Takoma Park, Maryland. Born in 1939, the son of a US public health service employee, Fahey had an unhappy childhood and turned to the radio for solace. In 1954 he heard Bill Monroe's version of Jimmie Rodgers' 'Blue Yodel No.7,' which he claims changed his life forever. Another formative tune was Blind Willie Johnson's 'Praise God I'm Satisfied,' a song which made him weep.

Fahey went on to graduate studies in folklore

and mythology at the University of California in Los Angeles. As part of his 'research,' Fahey tracked down the 'missing' blues artists Bukka White and Skip James. Skip James, at the time, had lost interest in music but was tired of work as a tenant farmer. So in 1964 he joined in with the folk revivalists and revived his own career.

In 1959 Fahey recorded his first album, with money he had earned from pumping gas. He made 95 copies. One side of the plain white wrapper said 'John Fahey', and the other said 'Blind Joe Death,' an invented blues artist about whom Fahey made up an entire mythology.

Fahey then started Takoma Records, whose artists included the young Leo Kottke and Peter Lang. It almost seemed that starting his own company was necessary, since his eccentricities led him to assimilate such diverse sources as classical, Indian ragas, blues and bluegrasss – an unlikely mix that a record company would have a hard time labeling, let alone promoting.

Somehow, all these influences mixed into a musical stew that left the listener engaged if not totally changed by the experience. Even though Fahey drew on the early blues artists for inspiration, he claims that in his music he hears grief and sadness, while in the blues artists he hears anger and humor.

Fahey called his style of guitar 'American Primitive.' Guitarist and guitar teacher Les Weller describes the style:

> "American Primitive guitar is grounded in our complex melting-pot American musical traditions. Hymns, rags, folk songs, jazz, classical, opera, eastern rhythms, contemporary tunes, and a galaxy of other musical sources contribute to this diverse form. Technique is based on using the multiple strings of the guitar to present the melody or theme supported by harmony and bass tones played simultaneously. Alternating bass is a regular feature, used in many forms to create a syncopation to support or contrast with other elements of the pieces. Varied tunings of the guitar enhance the instrument's tone, the playing of open strings reinforcing root tones and making multi-string techniques more accessible."

Fahey's eccentricities gave him an aura of mystery; and his penchant for drinking onstage gave his performances a certain unpredictability. He was said to have turned his back on his audience from time to time while performing on stage. It is said that his record sales actually went down after public appearances.

An American original, Fahey lived his life like he played his music. He disappeared from public performances, survived three divorces, wound up homeless and in the end died from complications from heart surgery. Still, he paved the way for artists such as Leo Kottke and Peter Finger and started a renaissance for acoustic guitar playing.

SONG: 'Steel Guitar Rag.'

GUITARS: various Gibson acoustics.

Leo Kottke

The 1969 release of Leo Kottke's *6- and 12-String Guitar* came like a breath of fresh air for

acoustic guitar fanatics who loved the sound of acoustic guitar but didn't care for the jangly associations of the post-folk hippie revival. It was as if Leo had swallowed a bunch of old blues albums and a bottle of amphetamines at the same time. The music on that album seemed to set out to make a point: let's infuse acoustic guitar with the energy of rock'n'roll but keep the rural sensibilities of early blues. Listening to the album for the first time is like going for a hayride. Leo's adrenaline-infused guitar instrumentals, combined with his onstage dry wit and beautiful renditions of compositions such as Bach's 'Jesu, Joy of Man's Desiring' made him the biggest success in the world of acoustic guitar virtuosos. Many a college dorm in 1969 was filled with the stale smoke of marijuana and young men scratching their heads saying, "How'd he do that?"

Early in his career Kottke aligned himself with John Fahey's Takomo label. The two seemed like a compatible duo, yet there are marked differences in their approaches. Kottke is more accessible and 'amped-up,' whereas Fahey is more moody, slower, and more wistful. Both are wonderful slide players. On Kottke's 'Vaseline Machine Gun' he establishes a driving, almost relentless groove based on the lower strings, then breaks into a slide phrase combined with an alternating bass that keeps the stew cooking. 'Watermelon,' another testosterone-driven tune, has such an uplifting feel you would have a hard time sitting down.

Kottke forgoes single string runs in favor of working his slide-playing around a solid bass-driven groove.

Nobody outside of Leadbelly has done as much to further the popularity of the 12-string guitar. Kottke made his name by exploring the tonalities of this instrument and if you have never played slide on a 12-string it is a real treat. The key is to use medium to heavy gauge strings and tune the guitar down. Kottke often tunes his guitar two to three half steps down. This will increase the 'growl factor' of your guitar and is essential for recreating the chunky sound as opposed to the more airy sound of the standard folk-oriented 12-string guitar.

Later recordings by Kottke tend to have a little less 'starch' but are well worthwhile even though he seems to have left the slide behind.
SONG: 'Vaseline Machine Gun.'
GUITARS: Taylor 6- and 12-strings.

Rock'n'roll

ROCK'N'ROLL IS ESSENTIALLY an amalgam of blues styles, including electric country blues, Kansas City blues, and Chicago and New Orleans blues. Chuck Berry and Bo Diddley introduced sounds from Chicago blues, while Fats Domino and Little Richard introduced elements of New Orleans blues. Rock pumped up the volume, speed and excitement of blues.

In rock'n'roll the electric guitar became king, president and prime minister. With its increased volume and sustain, as well as string-bending and distortion, the guitar could go places that it hadn't gone before. It became a more evocative instrument, duplicating the sound of the voice as well as horns and other instruments. Slide playing also evolved. With distortion came an infinite sustain that gave slide phrases a rawness and immediacy that the earlier acoustic bottleneck playing only hinted at.

Interestingly enough, a discussion of rock'n'roll, and specifically slide guitar in rock, harks back to the ubiquitous Robert Johnson. In 1961 an album of Johnson's recordings (recorded in 1936 and 1937) was released with little fanfare. Nevertheless, Johnson became a minor pop star. During his lifetime only 12 songs had been released and none, except 'Terraplane Blues,' sold particularly well.

But with the release of *King Of The Delta Blues Singers* in 1961, a new generation was becoming cognizant of the blues man who had been cut off in his prime. On the cover of Bob Dylan's *Bringing It All Back Home* (1965) was a photo of miscellaneous bohemian 'stuff,' including *King of the Delta Blues Singers* featured prominently. Eric Clapton, all of 15 or 16 years old when the album came out, remembers, "I don't think I'd even heard of Robert Johnson when I found the record… It was a real shock that there was something that powerful. It all led me to believe that there was this guy who really didn't want to play for people at all, that this thing was so unbearable for him to have to live with that he was almost ashamed of it. This was an image I was very, very keen to hang on to."

> ❝Johnson's raw emotion lent itself to the young generation's disenchantment with the establishment. He dared to ask questions.❞

Clapton's feelings, although very personal, struck a chord with anti-establishment youth. In Johnson's singing and playing was an anguish; a search for fulfillment of desires so overpowering that to attain them seemed impossible. For the up and coming rockers, Johnson's playing and anguish were akin to their own feelings of dissatisfaction. Johnson's music was thrilling and fearful; just the recipe for people bored with the complacency of middle-class life.

For the young generation this was *new* music. It helped that there was the mythical aspect of Johnson's life and his 'mysterious' death. Was he really killed? How was he killed? Poisoned? Stabbed? Did he sell his soul to the devil, as bluesmen like Son House used to say to explain away his amazing talent? Johnson's raw emotion lent itself to the young generation's disenchantment with the establishment. Robert Johnson dared to ask questions: What is a man's place in this world? Why is he cursed to want more than he can have?

Johnson was also relatively young when he recorded. He didn't have the wisdom and dignity of older bluesmen such as Son House and Skip James. In Johnson's recordings there is an element of shock that is lacking from the elder statesmen of blues.

There is also the musical complexity of Johnson's music, requiring more than one person could bring to it. Keith Richards recalls a visit to his art school pal, Brian Jones: "I'd just met

Brian, and I went round to his apartment – crash pad, actually. All he had in it was a chair, a record player, and a few records, one of which was Robert Johnson. He put it on and it was astounding stuff... To me he was like a comet or a meteor that came along and BOOM, suddenly he raised the ante. Suddenly you just had to aim that much higher."

British blues

THE BRITISH INVASION OF THE 1960S helped Americans discover their own music. While America was feasting on Elvis, doo-wop bands and surf music, British youth were discovering the old bluesmen. Brian Jones, Keith Richards, Eric Clapton, Jimmy Page, Jeff Beck, George Harrison, and Peter Green could all trace their inspiration back to the blues.

Part of what helped inspire these musicians was the series of American Folk Blues Festivals held in Europe between 1962 and 1970. The impact of huge music festivals such as Woodstock, Monterey Pop, and The Newport Folk Festival is hard to deny. However, of equal, if not more, importance – for the British and indirectly the US as well – were the American Folk Blues Festivals. Here, young British musicians like Mick Jagger, Brian Jones, and Jimmy Page were given first-hand exposure to some of the leading early bluesmen. It must have been incredible to hear Lonnie Johnson playing an electric guitar in 1963, Mississippi Fred McDowell playing slide on electric, and John Lee Hooker, looking confident if not a little scary, strutting out an incredible version of 'Hobo Blues.'

There was a burgeoning blues scene in England, but it was small and had yet to fully establish itself. The sole English show in the first year of the festival, at the Manchester Free Trade Hall in 1962, was more of a word-of-mouth affair, but attracted the likes of Jagger and Richards. At the end it was all chaos, with people everywhere... The festival was originally designed to be a single tour, but was so successful it prompted future bookings.

The musicians were treated like royalty and the show, while being a bit staged, was a class act. "The first time I went to Europe was 1962," says John Lee Hooker, in his biography *Boogie Man*, "and boy it was just like the President or Jesus comin' in... Every night was a sellout. Standing room only, no matter how big the place was." The musicians dressed in suits and the stage was decorated with images of Delta towns and the rural South.

Blues in England began to hit the charts and more press was devoted to the blues. The fledgling publication *Blues Unlimited*, founded in 1963 was becoming increasingly popular, and *Melody Maker*, which previously had only covered jazz, began to devote more space to blues.

The festival brought acts like Lightnin' Hopkins, Howlin' Wolf, Willie Dixon and Sonny Boy Williamson onto the European Stage. The Rolling Stones even decided to cover Wolf's 'Little Red Rooster,' releasing it as their fifth UK single. The single, featuring Brian Jones's

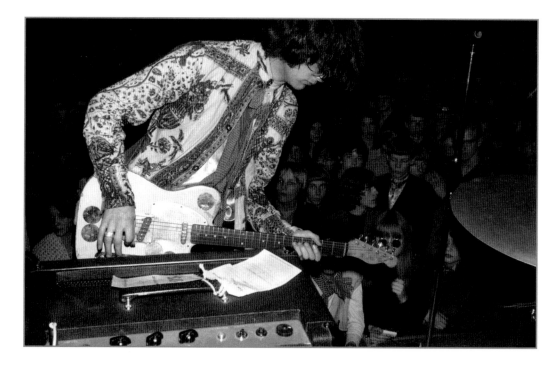

slide work, raced to number one on the charts and cemented the love affair England has had with American blues ever since.

The Yardbirds

Jimmy Page (above) was an early innovator (and blues aficionado), and Jeff Beck continues to be an innovative voice in the world of guitar. But of all the guitar heroes produced by the 1960s group The Yardbirds, it is Eric Clapton who continually pays tributes to his blues roots. From his early days in John Mayall's Blues Breakers, covering Freddie King's 'Hideaway,' to his 2004 tribute to Robert Johnson, *Me and Mr Johnson*, Clapton has proven his mettle as a 21st-century spokesman for the blues. He is not known as a slide player as such, but his collaborations with Allman Brothers guitarist Duane Allman helped bring to public awareness an incredible music talent. He has consistently brought blues musicians to the fore and made the rest of us take note of his influences.

Jimmy Page

A discussion of rock guitarists hardly seems appropriate without mentioning Jimmy Page. While Led Zeppelin innovated in the world of heavy metal and rock, they consistently drew on the early blues recordings for inspirations. Page was often dipping into the well of Robert Johnson and Elmore James riffs. His use of slide, however, was only one color in his sonic palette. One could say that Page's true genius was in the way he mixed sounds from all kinds of guitars and styles of playing (also, as producer of all the Led Zeppelin albums he is to be highly commended). Page could play boogie, Celtic finger-style, blues, and jazz-infused flourishes. His early recordings helped define the intense distorted rock sound that would become synonymous with Heavy Metal.

His sound featured a Fender Telecaster and Vox AC30 amplifiers – moving on to the Les Paul and Marshall 100-watt stacks of later Zeppelin recordings. He blended acoustic guitar, open tunings, mandolin, theremin, and of course a violin bow across the string of an electric guitar.

Page began playing guitar at the age of 15. Along with his friend, Jeff Beck, he played in pickup bands around England. His poor health (bouts of fatigue) confined him to the studio, where he became an in-demand session player, appearing on albums by The Who, The Rolling Stones, Donovan, Joe Cocker, and other popular British artists. The Yardbirds asked him to join, but instead he recommended Jeff Beck. Finally, in 1966 he did join the Yardbirds, but as their bassist. The union lasted two years and the band broke up. Page enlisted a friend from the session scene, bassist John Paul Jones, and teamed up with vocalist Robert Plant and Plant's drummer friend, John Bonham. This new band called itself The New Yardbirds (to fulfill contractual obligations) and toured Scandinavia. Upon return to England they had changed their name to Led Zeppelin (thanks to Keith Moon's comment that they would go over like a "lead balloon.")

The early Zeppelin albums, in particular, leaned on early blues for inspiration. Page also used some innovative tunings, including DADGAD ('Black Mountain Side,' 'Kashmir') and CACGCE ('Friends,' 'Bon-Yr-Aur').

SONG: 'In My Time of Dying.'
GUITAR: Gibson Les Paul.

Brian Jones

Known mainly as one of the founding guitarists of The Rolling Stones along with Keith Richards, Brian Jones (below) was also a member of Britain's first all-white blues band: Blues Incorporated. While the constantly shifting ranks of the band included most of the original

members of The Rolling Stones, it also included such luminaries as Ginger Baker and Jack Bruce. The Stones actually evolved out of this band and went on to incorporate more rockin' sounds into their mix. However, the blues sound continued to influence The Stones' writing. With other bands, such as The Yardbirds, Savoy Brown, and Ten Years After, they established a new genre: blues-rock.

In the early days, Jones held down the lion's share of The Stones' rhythm and slide playing, while Richards handled most of the lead work. Richards' Chuck Berry-influenced playing showed on covers of 'Route 66' and 'Carol,' while Jones' triplet-based licks sparked up Elmore James-style tunes like 'Little Red Rooster,' and 'I Wanna Be Your Man.'

Towards the end of the 1960s, Jones became less interested in the guitar and took up the sitar, dulcimer and marimba, leaving the bulk of guitar playing on Stones records to Richards. In 1969 Jones left the Stones to pursue a solo career. A month later he drowned in his swimming pool.

If Keith Richards helped a new generation appreciate Chuck Berry, it was Jones who is owed thanks for helping introduce Elmore James and Robert Johnson to British blues devotees. He strayed from these roots – and in doing so he inspired some of the Stones more creative and experimental efforts – but the early recordings do firmly establish him as one of England's founding white blues musicians.

SONG: 'Little Red Rooster.'
GUITAR: Vox 'teardrop.'

George Harrison

'My Sweet Lord' has some of the most wistful, memorable (and infinitely hummable) slide licks around. The slide work on The Beatles' 'Something' is beautiful; like most of Harrison's guitar work it is simple, unique and representative of the man's incredible talent. The 'quiet' Beatle was not only a tremendous guitarist but a great songwriter in his own right – even though Lennon/McCartney got most of the accolades.

The youngest Beatle, born in 1943, Harrison grew up in a strict household and had to sneak out of the house to play his first gig with his brother, Peter. He rode the bus to school with his friend, Paul McCartney, and the two would often stop off at each others' houses to listen to records. George was too young at 14 to join Paul's group, The Quarrymen, but he hung out with the group and emulated his hero, John Lennon. Eventually, well, you know what happened... Ed Sullivan, screaming girls, *A Hard Day's Night...* Maharishi Mahesh Yogi... Eric Clapton steals his wife... *All Things Must Pass*...a brilliant solo career... Traveling Wilburys... an unsuccessful battle with cancer... We miss him dearly.

The spiritual center of The Beatles, Harrison was responsible for introducing the group to a varied palette of musical influences, just as Brian Jones had with The Rolling Stones. Those influences included the Indian sitar and, of course, slide guitar. Harrison's early influences were Carl Perkins and Andres Segovia. He worked hard to master a precise picking technique that would become useful in his sitar arrangements.

Harrison's playing was never big on histrionics. Instead he used subtle and catchy guitar lines. His lead playing always played to the song. Of course, the Beatles were never a jam band. Songwriting was brought to a level that has gone unsurpassed since the inception of the Fab Four. All musical expression was in the service of the song. Even with George Martin at the helm of The Beatles' recordings, it is the songs, melodies and lyrical content that we all remember.

Even as a solo artist, Harrison never went the route of other lead guitarists: putting his chops above his art. An understated player, he sought a higher ground, where all things would pass...

SONGS: 'Something,' 'My Sweet Lord.'
GUITAR: Fender Stratocaster.

Rod Price

One of my most vivid sonic memories of the 1970s is the sound of Foghat's 'Slowride' coming on the radio as we were headed down the road towards teenage oblivion. Rod Price's slide work on the track felt like it was coming apart at the seams, which was emblematic of our own lives. We survived, and so did Rod (Dave Peverett, Foghat's vocalist and second guitar player, however, passed away from cancer in February, 2000.) No other player comes to mind who represents the sheer wildness of rock slide playing like Price.

Price's first introduction to guitar was hearing Big Bill Broonzy on the radio. Then came Scrapper Blackwell, Elmore James, Robert Johnson and Muddy Waters, all of whom inspired Rod to play the blues-flavored music he loved.

His first band, Shakey Big City Blues Band, was heralded by Champion Jack Dupree as "the best blues band in Europe." One of his next projects was Black Cat Bones, where he replaced Paul Kossoff (founding guitarist of Free, the 1970s band). In Foghat, he was dubbed "the magician of slide." Three platinum and eight gold records later Rod has become a bona fide star.

Foghat was founded in 1971 by Price and 'Lonesome' Dave Peverett on vocals and second guitar, Roger Earl on drums and Tony Stevens on bass. The band cut its teeth on Chicago-based blues by artists like Willie Dixon, but its big hits came with originals: 'Fool For the City,' 'I Just Want to Make Love to You,' and the aforementioned 'Slow Ride.' Their music suffered somewhat from 1970s era bombast, but Price's slide playing is still worth listening to. They reached their height in 1977 with the release of *Foghat Live*, but in the 1980s they fell into obscurity. Various incarnations lasted until Peverett's death in 2000.

Price has carried on and has released several solo recordings. Over the years he has worked with John Lee Hooker, Muddy Waters, and several other blues artists.

SONG: 'Slow Ride.'

GUITAR: Gibson Les Paul.

Rory Gallagher

Rory Gallagher (right) is probably best known for producing straight-ahead blues-flavored rock. During the mid 1970s, when arena rock was in vogue and bands seem to favor performances and recordings of an epic nature, Gallagher's stripped-down format was a breath of fresh air. He played the most beat-up 1959 Stratocaster on the planet and his penchant for wearing plaid shirts reinforced his image as the working man's guitarist. A fiery player who blended blues sensibilities with rock'n'roll excitement, Gallagher was a player first and a rock star second. Known for his friendly demeanor, he kept up a touring pace in the early 1970s that would have killed most people and nearly exhausted his band.

He first came to the attention of the world during the mid-1960s in a band called Taste. Taste, a power trio, blended American blues with the new sounds of heavy metal. The band broke up in 1971 and Gallagher went solo. He began to garner a big following in Europe and the United States. While Gallagher did not pioneer any particular sounds – unlike contemporaries such as Jimmy Page and Jeff Beck – he gave an excitement to blues-driven rock albums like *Against the Grain* and *Photo Finish*. His slide playing is reminiscent of Elmore James with a shot of adrenaline.
SONG: 'Souped Up Ford.'
GUITAR: Fender Stratocaster.

Meanwhile, back in the USA...

THANKS, IN PART, TO THEIR BRITISH counterparts, Americans were rediscovering their own music: the blues.

Duane Allman

Duane Allman's short but explosive career would not only help define the roots of Southern rock, but his slide playing became the pinnacle to which guitar players then and now would aspire.

Born in Tennessee in 1946, Duane moved to Daytona Beach, Florida, in 1957 with his family. His younger brother, Greg, took up the guitar, but Duane was so enthralled with the instrument he had Greg teach him how to play. Eventually, the older brother became more proficient on the instrument and the younger boy moved to keyboards.

The two brothers played in a band called The House Rockers, backing up a black vocal group, The Untils. Next, they formed a band called The Allman Joys, recorded a single ('Spoonful'), and began touring the southern club circuit. Eventually, the band broke up and

the Allmans formed a new band, Hour Glass, which made it out to California and opened for bands such as The Doors. This band also did not garner much commercial success and broke up. Greg stayed in Los Angles and Duane (right) remained in the South, jamming with several musicians who would eventually become The Allman Brothers.

In 1968 Duane played a session with Wilson Pickett, recording the Beatles 'Hey Jude,' which went on to become a huge hit for Pickett. Duane was then asked to join the Muscle Shoals Rhythm Section, and played on recordings with Aretha Franklin and Boz Scaggs. In 1969 Allman's contract was sold to Capricorn Records. Phil Walden, who ran the company, wanted Allman to put together a band. From various jams, Allman put together a band and asked his brother to join on organ and lead vocals. The Allman Brothers' first album didn't reach very far on the charts, but it established the band's heavyweight instrumental prowess. Twin guitar parts, harmonized leads played by Allman and Dickey Betts, became the signature sound for The Allman Brothers Band.

In the fall of 1970, Duane participated in another session with guitarist Eric Clapton. The album, a one-shot affair, was called *Layla and Other Assorted Love Songs*, and the band was called Derek & The Dominoes. The playing of these two giants of guitar on this record is one for the ages.

Back with The Allman Brothers Band in 1971, Duane recorded a live two-record set called *Live at Fillmore East*. The set featured one of Allman's best recorded examples of slide playing on the opener, 'Statesboro Blues.'

In the fall of 1971, The Allman Brothers returned to the studio. They completed the tracks: 'Stand Back,' 'Blue Sky,' and Duane's lovely acoustic original, 'Little Martha.' Unfortunately, while the band was taking a break from recording, Duane Allman was killed in a motorcycle accident. His legacy lives on, inspiring a new generation of guitarists such as Sonny Landreth and Warren Haynes and pretty much anybody else who decided to play slide guitar after 1969.

SONG: 'Statesboro Blues.'
GUITAR: Fender Stratocaster.

Warren Haynes

It wasn't until the early 1990s that The Allman Brothers were able to replace guitarist Duane Allman. The man who would have to fill some mighty big shoes was Warren Haynes. He played in the spirit of Allman but added his own jazz-influenced runs. The Allman Brothers, who had been sagging in popularity, regained much of their lost fan base with Haynes at the helm. Haynes was able to meld his blues-based slide playing convincingly with the more melodic approach of founder Dickie Betts. He formed his own band, Gov't Mule, which drew much of its inspiration from Haynes' blues-based playing. At the beginning of the 21st century, Haynes found himself filling some more big shoes, those of Jerry Garcia of The Grateful Dead. With the passing of Garcia, it was thought that the other members of The Dead would hang it up. But just to prove you can't keep a good man down, or a good band down, the remaining members decided to ask Haynes to join them in 2004. A man who seems to breathe new life into once great bands is a man to be reckoned with.

SONG: 'Statesboro Blues.'

GUITAR: Gibson Les Paul.

Johnny Winter

Johnny Winter was born February 23rd, 1944, in Beaumont, Texas. Beaumont, at the time, was a city rife with racial tensions and had been the site of one of the worst race riots in Texas history, just nine months before Winter's birth. Businesses were burned and martial law went into effect as 2,000 National Guardsmen and Texas Rangers sealed off the town from the rest of the world. Winter (right), however, was sincere in his love of blues music, and was welcomed into the black community.

He became friends with Clarence Garlow, a local DJ at the black radio station KJET, who introduced Winter to rural blues and Cajun music. In 1962, the story goes, Winter and his musician brother, Edgar, went to see B.B. King at a local blues club. Edgar and Johnny were the only whites in the crowd, and Johnny wanted to get up on stage and play. King was reluctant, and wanted to see the young man's union card, which Winter showed him. Still not sure about this young white kid, King was finally convinced by several people in the crowd to let the boy play. Winter played, got a standing ovation and King grabbed his guitar back.

Johnny got his breakthrough in 1968, when *Rolling Stone* magazine

LOWELL GEORGE (RIGHT) WITH PAUL BARRÈRE IN LITTLE FEAT

ran an article on the Texas music scene. A bidding war broke out, won by Columbia Records. On his first album, released in 1969, he covered songs by Robert Johnson, Sonny Boy Williamson II and B.B. King. In addition to recording several more blues-based albums, Winter helped reintroduce blues legend Muddy Waters to a new generation of listeners by producing and playing on three albums in the late 1970s and early 1980s. Waters and Winters friendship evolved to the point that Waters would refer to Johnny as his adopted son.

Winter plays rockin' blues in the Texas tradition, mean and nasty with a lot of swing.
SONGS: 'It's My Life, Baby.'
GUITAR: Gibson Firebird.

Lowell George

Between 1969 and 1979, Lowell George, playing with Little Feat and others, built up a reputation as one of the premier slide guitarists of his day. He drew on sources as varied as New Orleans R&B, rock, Latin, Celtic and Asian in his playing. He played on recordings with artists such as John Sebastian, The Meters, Carly Simon, and The Grateful Dead.

> **"While Allman's solos were blues-based, Lowell George used influences from around the world."**

In the late 1960s, George (opposite right, with Paul Barrère in Little Feat) hooked up with Frank Zappa and the Mothers of Invention, recording two albums, *Cruising with Rueben and the Jets* and *Weasels Rip My Flesh*. He left Zappa's band to form Little Feat in 1971. The band had little success with its first three albums, but 1974's *Feats Don't Fail Me Now* cracked the charts and established George as an incredible slide player. His slide work on 'Rock and Roll Doctor,' 'Oh Atlanta,' and 'Cold, Cold Cold/Triple Face Boogie' are particularly notable.

Little Feat broke up in 1977 and George pursued a solo career. His health, unfortunately, was faltering. Suffering from hepatitis, he nonetheless recorded an album, *Thanks, I'll Eat It Here*, and toured in support of it. During the tour, however, he suffered a heart attack and was pronounced dead on June 29th, 1979.

Compared to Duane Allman's robust slide style, George played more in support of the song. Allman's solos were predominantly blues-based, while George used influences from around the globe to color his playing. He was also an excellent singer and songwriter.
SONG: 'Dixie Chicken.'
GUITAR: Fender Stratocaster.

Billy Gibbons

Billy Gibbons, the long-bearded guitarist for ZZ Top, was born on either March 4th or December 16th, 1950 and was raised in and around Houston, Texas. He grew up in a household full of classical and country music, but was transformed – as so many young impressionable musicians of the time were – by an appearance of Elvis Presley on the Ed Sullivan television show. Receiving a Gibson Melody Maker guitar and Fender Champ amplifier for his 13th birthday, the youngster was soon emulating heroes like Little Richard and Jimmy Reed. He played in a series of bands playing psychedelic rock and pop tunes during the mid- to late-1960s. Jimi Hendrix, who had Gibbons' band, The Moving Sidewalks, open for him on a Texas tour, called Billy one of his favorite up-and-coming guitarists.

In 1969 he formed a band with bassist Dusty Hill and drummer Frank Beard, forgoing the earlier pop sound for a more straight forward rockin' blues sound. The band was ZZ Top, and it has kept the same lineup since its inception. It released a series of albums in the early- to mid-1970s (including its self-titled debut, *Rio Grande Mud, Tres Hombres, Fandango,* and *Tejas*), becoming one of the country's biggest rock draws. After a three-year hiatus, Top came back in the 1980s with a reworked sound, using sequenced bass, electronic drums and synthesizers. This new direction seem to turn off some hard-core fans, but led to commercial successes such as, 'Legs,' 'Sharp Dressed Man' and 'Give Me All Your Lovin.''

Some of Gibbons' best slide playing can be heard on the 1974 hit, 'Tush.'

SONG: 'Tush.'
GUITAR: Gibson Les Paul.

Ry Cooder

Ry Cooder was given a guitar at the age of ten. It became his driving passion to the exclusion of pretty much anything else. His politically radical upbringing introduced him to the music of Woody Guthrie, and the mythological aspects of Guthrie's concern with the 'dust bowl' and the rural poor struck a strong chord. But it was Delta-style blues that he found even more alluring. He cites 'Dark was the Night, Cold was the Ground' as the inspiration for the memorable theme to his soundtrack for Wim Wenders' film *Paris, Texas*.

The young native Californian would soak up performances from Sleepy John Estes and Reverend Gary Davis, steeping himself in blues traditions being performed by the last remaining original practitioners of the style.

In his early career he was a sought-after session man, having recorded tracks with The Rolling Stones. In 1970 he recorded his first solo album. Ry Cooder is known for blending myriad traditional sounds into his music, including rural blues, Brazilian and Hawaiian: he traveled to Hawaii to study slack-key guitar with Gabby Pahinui, and spent six months learning the accordion so he could play with Flaco Jimenez, the Mexican master.

Cooder's film score credits include *Southern Comfort*, *The Long Riders*, *The Border* and *Paris, Texas*. His sound is haunting and distinctive. His music lends itself so well to film partly because he composes in such a visual manner; one can almost see the rural landscapes of swamps with dark forbidding places, undercurrents of menace in a stark and beautiful landscape. Many modern players cite Ry Cooder as their inspiration for learning slide guitar. They couldn't have a better example of great slide playing. Using heavy-gauged strings and numerous different tunings, Cooder gives the sound the breadth and tone it deserves.

SONG: 'Dark Was The Night.'

GUITARS: Gibson Roy Smeck model from the mid 1930s; 1950s Martin 000-18; Fender Stratocaster.

TUNINGS: Spanish (DGDGBD).

Bonnie Raitt

Few women have made a name for themselves as guitarists in the blues-rock field. Bonnie Raitt (opposite) is the exception. Previously lumped in with folkies such as Jackson Browne and The Eagles, Raitt began her recording career in the early 1970s. Initially, she was more highly regarded for her sultry voice than her fine guitar licks.

Raitt, however was raised on the country blues of Mississippi Fred McDowell and the Chicago blues of Muddy Waters. She sought out the old masters, collecting records while still a student at Radcliffe College in Massachusetts. In the late 1960s she quit college and began playing the bar circuit, making it out to California. Her early recordings had some fine slide work and her signature gravelly singing stood out. But she was never mainstream enough for her label, Warner Bros, and so she switched to Capitol, where she flexed her blues muscles.

It was a good move, because she scored a Number One album with 1989's *Nick of Time*. The album sports the John Hiatt tune, 'Thing Called Love,' featuring Raitt's electric slide work. That same year she walked away with four Grammy awards for *Nick of Time*. The follow-up album, *Luck of the Draw*, featured the hit 'Something to Talk About,' with its lazy slide lines and sexually charged vocal. She has gone on to record collaborations with John Lee Hooker, Roy Orbison, and BB King, to name but a few.

SONG: 'Something to Talk About.'
GUITAR: 1969 Fender Stratocaster.

> "Bay Area guitarist Roy Rogers has made a name for himself by playing slide exclusively."

Roy Rogers

San Francisco Bay Area slide guitarist Roy Rogers has done what few other guitarists have done: made a name for himself by playing slide guitar exclusively. Whether playing his 1970 Martin O-16 acoustic, or his Gibson ES-125, three-quarter scale electric, his music is imbued with the energy of rock and the swampy textures of New Orleans blues.

Born in 1950 in Redding, California, the young Rogers grew up in Vallejo and started playing guitar at age 12. By age 16, he had become increasingly influenced by Delta blues, particularly Robert Johnson. He formed an acoustic duet with harp player David Burgin in 1973. Later, in 1980, he formed the Delta Rhythm Kings, playing numerous gigs at San Francisco's oldest blues bar, The Saloon. Early in the 1980s, Rogers teamed up with John Lee Hooker and toured for four years with The Coast to Coast Blues Band.

Rogers also went on to produce several albums by Hooker, including *The Healer, Mr. Lucky* and *Boom Boom*. By 1986 he was able to record his first solo album, *Chops Not Chaps*. He has gone on to record several solo albums, including the all-instrumental *Slideways*.

He achieves his distinctive sound by running his signal through a chorus pedal with a gain boost. He wears a short slide, which he says leaves the other three fingers free for fretting chords. The sound is amplified by a Mesa Boogie Mark II and a Leslie amp.

SONG: 'Avalanche.'
GUITAR: Gibson ES-125, Martin 0-16.

Sonny Landreth

Sonny Landreth might be considered slightly under the radar as modern slide guitarists go, but that is because he is better known as a sideman in other people's bands, such as those of John Hiatt and Clifton Chenier: he was the first white man to play in Chenier's band. He is, however, not only a great slide player but an accomplished singer and songwriter.

Born in Canton, Mississippi (the home of another great slide player, Elmore James), Landreth moved to Colorado before returning to Mississippi where he joined several Cajun bands, including Beausoleil and Chenier's band. In the 1980s he joined John Hiatt on the songwriting master's *Slow Turning* album. It was here that Landreth really began to make a name for himself, using his wonderful single-string melodies along with a percussive attack that set him apart from many slide players. While his playing has been compared to that of Ry Cooder and David Lindley, his blend of Cajun, rock, and blues gives him a distinctive voice in the slide field. He favors A, A minor, Asus, C, D minor, E, and G tunings.
SONG: 'Taylor's Rock.'

GUITARS: Gibson Les Paul, Fender Stratocaster.

EQUIPMENT: Sonny uses a Transperformer on his Les Paul, a computer-driven device that allows him to change tunings at the touch of a button. He runs his guitar through a Fulltone Fulldrive 2 distortion pedal or a Big Muff, along with a Boss CE-5 chorus run through a 75 watt Demeter amp head and a Marshall 4x12 cabinet.

David Lindley

Similar to Ry Cooder in his eclectic tastes, David Lindley is as much known for his guitar prowess – most notably lap-steel type solos – as he is for melding ethnic music such as ska, reggae, African, and calypso. He came to the attention of the world through his collaborations with folk artist Jackson Browne. He appeared on several albums by Browne in the 1970s, including *For Everyman* (1973), *Late for the Sky* (1974), *The Pretender* (1976), and *Running on Empty* (1977). The last album helped define his sound with the song 'The Loadout/Stay,' with its lap steel guitar solo resembling a distorted bottleneck.

His 1981 solo project, *El-Rayo X*, kept on the Lindley tradition of eclecticism, but it was the full-throttle 'Mercury Blues' that raced through with more bottleneck-style playing (actually played on lap steel). In addition to working with Jackson Browne, Lindley has been a sideman for Rod Stewart, Linda Ronstadt, and Crosby & Nash.

Lindley has a penchant for cheap guitars. He favors Sears Silvertones and funky lap steel guitars over the standard Stratocaster and Les Paul.

SONG: 'Mercury Blues.'

GUITARS: all kinds of weird stuff.

Sacred Steel

IN THE LATE 1930S, THE ELECTRIC steel guitar was introduced into the African-American church by brothers Troman and Willie Eason. The instrument has continued to evolve within the church over the past 60 years and has become an incredible voice in gospel music.

Powered by spiritual worship and an energy that is infectious, this is a style of slide playing that is woefully under-represented in the secular community. Naturally, the music is played in the service of a 'higher' authority, but even for atheists and agnostics it has a lot to offer, including some of the best slide playing around.

Brought to the attention of the secular world by Chris Strachwitz and Arhoolie Records, the Sacred Steel series has given players like Robert Randolph their own reputation outside the church service.

The music's geographical center is the state of Florida, but also includes musicians from Seattle, Detroit and Rochester, New York. The leader of the current movement to bring sacred steel players together is Marcus Hardy.

Playing his steel guitar at The House of God church in Crescent City, Florida, for groups of a dozen or so holy worshippers, Hardy had a dream to create a community of steel players; one that could share their love of God and music and showcase their talents for each other. In March 2000, his dream came true when the first Annual Sacred Steel Convention was held at Rollins College in Winter Park, Florida.

The image of a steel guitar in a church service for African-Americans seems bizarre, especially since that instrument has become more closely associated with white players and country music. But the instrument, often a replacement for the more common organ, has the ability to whip a congregation into a frenzy. Notable players include Robert Randolph, Aubrey Ghent, and the Campbell Brothers.

Many of the sacred steel players utilize an E7 tuning. Here are two possible versions of that: BDEG#BE (low to high); and BEG#BDE. By way of contrast, here is an E tuning: EBEG#BE (low to high).

Steel guitar, country music and guit-steel

WHEN THE NATIONAL AND DOBRO resonator guitars arrived on the scene in the late 1920s, they were offered in square-neck and round-neck versions. The round-neck style was meant to be played like a regular guitar. The square-neck guitars, however, were meant to be played on the player's lap. Soon, electronics began to play a bigger role in amplified music and pickups were added to the guitar. Problems arose with feedback, and so hollow-body guitars were replaced by solid-bodies.

Later, the lap steel evolved into a multi-neck instrument, with two, three, and sometimes four necks. With more physical bulk the instruments became virtually impossible to hold on your lap and so legs were added, thus creating the first 'console' instruments. Strings were added to some of the necks, and by the end of World War II the eight-string neck was fairly standard for console style lap steels.

In the early 1950s, players began experimenting with pedals that could raise the pitch of the string. In 1953 Bud Isaacs was the first player to use pedal steel on a hit recording: 'Slowly,' by Webb Pierce. Players would often devise their own tunings, but eventually E9 (Nashville tuning) and C6 (jazz) tuning seemed to become the standard and are probably the most popular setups today. Steel guitars have also evolved into 10- and even 12-string necks.

IMPORTANT PLAYERS: Speedy West, Pete Drake.

> **"The guit-steel combines a guitar neck with an eight-string lap steel tuned to a C13 chord."**

GUIT-STEEL
Junior Brown

"A lot of people tell me they don't like country music, but they like what I am doing," says Junior Brown of Austin, Texas. This seems a bit ironic, since his playing is steeped in old time country flavor. However, with Brown's hyper-kinetic 'guit-steel' playing, he also blends in the energy of rock'n'roll. The guit-steel was born in 1985 after Brown, who had been moving back and forth between lap steel and guitar while singing, decided he needed to wed the two. "I had this dream that the two just kinda melted together. When I woke up, I thought 'You know, that thing would work!' They make double-neck guitars and double-neck steels, so why not one of each?"

A double-neck guitar, the guit-steel combines the best of both worlds: the six-string guitar part is set up just like a Telecaster, and the steel part is an eight-string lap steel tuned to a C13 chord: Bb CEGACEG, low to high. Brown combines classic country lap steel runs with classic Telecaster sounds in his set. In *Guitar Player*'s 1994 polls he was voted Number One lap steel player, Number Two country artist and had the Number Three country album.

He began playing music in the early 1960s and by the end of the decade, still a teenager, he turned professional. His father was a piano player and there was always music in the house. His hero, at an early age, was Ernest Tubb, whom he later honored in his song, 'My Baby Don't Dance to Nothing But Ernest Tubb.' Brown was able to meet Tubb on several occasions and his advice to his young protégé was "keep it country."

In the 1980s, Brown was teaching guitar under Leon McAulliffe, the legendary steel player for Bob Wills' Texas Playboys, at Oklahoma's Hank Thompson School of Country Music, part of Rogers State College. It was here that he met the "lovely Tanya Rae" who would become his rhythm guitarist and wife.

Tanya Rae and Junior moved to Austin, Texas, where the musical lines between various styles are a bit blurry. In Brown's set you will hear a lot of old-time country, naturally, but you will also hear influences of surf and a bit of Jimi Hendrix. (It seems that once slide playing broke into two camps, bottleneck and lap steel, there developed lines that weren't crossed. The lap steel players created their own tunings and phrasing, while the bottleneck players pretty much stuck to what they had been doing.) Brown's playing, while not combining the two techniques, seems to open the door to a hybrid style of playing, where blues mixes effortlessly with country.

You can hear Brown rippin' it up on several CDs, but 1994's *Guit With It* is perhaps his best, with its great playing, Junior's wry wit ('You're Wanted By The Police And My Wife Thinks You're Dead') and lovely vocal interplay with Tanya Rae.

Slide guitar today

SLIDE GUITAR TODAY IS REPRESENTED by a host of great players who have used the style to embellish their songwriting and evoke the textures of a rural past. Ben Harper, Alvin Youngblood Hart, and Kelly Joe Phelps are artists who use a myriad of styles to create excellent songs; slide guitar is just one of the choices they make in creating sonic portraits. There are, however, still the virtuosi of slide guitar, those who have made a name for themselves based strictly on their abilities as players: Roy Rogers, Sonny Landreth, and Bob Brozman. There is also the Celtic-influenced playing of Martin Simpson, and the traditional blues sound of L'il Ed Williams.

Alvin Youngblood Hart

Some call him the Cosmic American Love Child of Howlin' Wolf and Link Wray, but it is his interpretations of old rural blues that have earned Alvin Youngblood Hart (opposite) the highest praise from artists such as Eric Clapton and Ben Harper. His debut recording *Big*

BEN HARPER

Mama's Door in 1996 proved that the waters of the Mississippi Delta ran deep in this young man. Born in 1963, he played songs from the repertoire of Charlie Patton and Robert Johnson like they were second nature to him.

Since the release of his first CD, he has gone on to record several other outings that keep pushing the boundaries of roots music. He is just as likely these days to pick up an electric guitar with tons of distortion as he is to pick up an acoustic and evoke the ghosts of Mississippi's past.

He was born in Oakland, California but moved all over the United States. As he puts it, "three high schools in three time zones." He spent seven years in the Coast Guard; three years as a grunt seaman on a buoy tender on the Lower Mississippi River, and three years as an electronics technician at a radio transmitter station on the West Coast. His electronics background has proved handy for fixing amplifiers in his wife's Memphis guitar shop.

> **"Some call Alvin the Cosmic American Love Child of Howlin' Wolf and Link Wray."**

Even though Hart seems to shrug off his label as a blues revivalist, he constantly receives accolades from the blues society at large. In 1997, he received the W.C. Handy award for best new blues artist. His 1998 release, *Territory*, received the *Downbeat* critics' poll award for best blues album – even though it wasn't a blues album. He also received the BBC's award of blues record of the year for his 2000 release, *Start With the Soul*. In 2003 he was nominated for a Grammy.

SONG: 'Joe Friday.'
GUITARS: various.

Ben Harper

Ben Harper (opposite) is a true 21st century journeyman. His music combines funky-soul and jam-band sensibilities with craftsmanlike attention to detail in songwriting. A native of California, Harper grew up listening to blues, folk, soul, R&B, and reggae. He started playing guitar as a youngster, and soon became proficient at acoustic slide, which has become his signature instrument. He is one of the few musicians today who plays a Weissenborn guitar: a lap-style guitar made of wood, with a hollow neck.

Playing steady gigs in the Los Angeles area, Harper scored a deal with Virgin records and released his first album *Welcome to the Cruel World* in 1994. His sophomore effort *Fight for Your Mind* was a politically heavy-hitting album with more musical experimentation.

In addition to his solo recordings, Harper has recorded with blues star John Lee Hooker and blues-rockers Gov't Mule.

SONG: 'Whipping Boy.'
GUITAR: Weissenborn lap-style.

Kelly Joe Phelps

Playing slide guitar on his lap – not a Dobro, National, or Weissenborn guitar, but a regular

old Dreadnought – in open D tuning makes Kelly Joe Phelps a bit of an anomaly in the guitar world. But then this guitarist/singer/songwriter is nothing if not original. His playing and songwriting are filled with virtuosity and mystique that come across like an Impressionist painting. There is a blur between lyric and musical phrasing; one colors the other, but neither can rest on its own. The two combine to leaves us in state of suspension. Listening to Kelly Joe Phelps, one is challenged to interpret his musical offerings in a very personal way.

Raised in the state of Washington, Phelps learned country and folk music, as well as piano and drums from his father. He soon began to concentrate on free jazz and came under the influence of such artists as Miles Davis, Ornette Coleman, and John Coltrane. In the 1980s he focused on acoustic blues and was inspired by players like Mississippi Fred McDowell and Robert Pete Williams.

'The House Carpenter,' from his 1999 release *Shine Eyed Mister Zen*, highlights Phelps's unique slide playing. The sound is pure wood, but the technique employed (lap-style) gives the song a different sound to traditional acoustic-style slide playing. He employs an alternating bass and finger-picking techniques. String-damping is critical to Phelps' style of playing. He plays in open D tuning: DADF#AD, low to high. If you wish to play like Phelps, try using some dobro-style techniques.

SONG: 'The House Carpenter.'
GUITAR: Gibson J-60.

Bob Brozman

A unique voice in the world of modern acoustic guitar is Bob Brozman (below left), a man steeped in the musical traditions of the world. Brozman's collaborations with artists from around the globe have included Hawaiian artist Ledward Kaapana, Indian slide player Debashish Bhattacharya, Japanese lute player Takashi Hirayasu (below right, with Brozman) and many others.

Brozman's background is also rich in the traditions of American roots music, including Delta blues and Hawaiian-style playing. He was born in New York in 1954 and started playing guitar at age six. He studied music and ethnomusicology at Washington University in St. Louis.

Moving to Santa Cruz, California, Brozman made his living playing on the streets, bars and clubs of the coastal town. Since then he has probably logged more miles on international flights than any other musician alive, spending significant time touring Europe, Asia, Africa, Australia, New Zealand, and South America. Along the way he has amassed many friends and collaborators. Bob is constantly injecting his rhythmic playing, combining elements of blues, jazz, Gypsy swing, calypso, and even modern hip-hop and ska, into the melting pot of world music.

He plays many National resonator guitars, and has been a big reason for the resurgence in the company and its instruments. He has even written a book on the subject, *The History and Artistry of National Resonator Instruments*. His slide playing combines many percussive elements as well as a bag full of tricks that leave the listener wondering what kind of effects

he is using. But there are none; it's 100 per cent natural. He is as well known for his take on Delta blues as he is for his slide playing in the Hawaiian style.

Comfortable with the guitar in standard position or playing slide with a square neck guitar on his lap, Bob truly has mastered the nuances of playing slide guitar.

SONG: 'Man Of Steel Blues.'

GUITAR: various National Tricones and single-cone guitars.

Martin Simpson

A beautiful voice in the world of acoustic fingerstyle guitar, Martin Simpson has continually added new colors to his palette, expanding on his primary interests in British, Anglo-American, and Afro-American traditional forms. Born May 1953 in Lincolnshire, England, Simpson started playing professionally in 1971. He recorded his first album, *Golden Vanity*, in 1976 and within a year he was opening shows for bands such as Steeleye Span. Through the years he has recorded many collaborations with singer June Tabor. In 1987 he moved to the United States and has lived there since.

In his music, Simpson has drawn on the inspiration of artists such as Henry Cox, Blind Willie Johnson, and Blind Willie McTell, as well as Bob Dylan and Richard Thompson. Martin's music is a reflection of both British and US regional influences. But like Bob Brozman, he has also incorporated world influences, from sources like Wu Man, the Chinese lute player, with whom he recorded *Music for the Motherless Child* in 1996. Simpson's playing is economical, concentrating his effort on making each note count. His slide playing is clean and articulate, substituting purity of soul for histrionics.

SONG: 'Greenfields Of Canada.'

GUITAR: Sobell acoustic.

Li'l Ed Williams

Li'l Ed and the Blues Imperials have been dubbed "the world's number one houserocking band." Williams, whom some would call 'petite,' is, however, a giant among blues slide players. Hailing from the West Side of Chicago, Williams boasts a direct bloodline to the great slide player, J.B Hutto (his uncle and musical mentor). The band is a favorite at blues festivals throughout the United States, and thanks to Williams' gifted vocals and on-stage flamboyance – a penchant for duck-walking and back-bending – has become a top blues act.

Born in 1955, Ed was surrounded by the blues. He was playing guitar, drums, and bass by the time he was 12 years old. Ed claims that his uncle, J.B Hutto, "taught me everything I know." By 1975 he had formed the first incarnation of The Blues

Imperials, playing every West Side club at night while he worked ten hours a day at a car wash. The band released its first album *Roughhousin'* in 1986. Since then Ed hasn't looked back to his car wash days.

As can be guessed, the Imperials play good-time-music and Ed's slide playing is a spirited amalgam of the styles of Chicago blues players like Elmore James and J.B. Hutto. Turn it up, get down and let it ride!

SONG: 'Never Miss Your Water.'
GUITAR: Gibson ES-335.

Slides and technique

TODAY SLIDES COME IN ALL SORTS of exotic shapes and sizes – some even rather suggestive. One's choice of slide is very much a personal decision. However, here are some tips for what kind of slide might best suit your needs. Keep in mind that you will probably want to buy a small assortment of slides to experiment with.

You can choose from metal/brass, glass, or ceramic slides; there might be other materials out there but these are the best. Glass tends to be a little smoother than metal but some people say metal is louder. I like the sound of brass, but unless the brass stays polished it has a tendency to get a little 'sticky.' These days I prefer ceramic, it seems to combine the best qualities of both metal and glass; it slides better on the string with a consistent pressure. The metal slides are thinner and therefore a bit easier to direct and get accuracy directly over the fret. If you go for glass I recommend a thicker glass to the thinner variety: thinner glass slides have a tendency to sound thin. You can also use household objects such as a socket from a socket wrench set or (a blues classic!) the cut-off top of a wine bottle .

PLACEMENT: Most players place the slide on their pinky; this gives you the most flexibility, allowing the other fingers freedom to fret other strings and make chords. There are, of course, many players (some of them presented in this book) who place the slide on their ring, middle or even their index finger. The slide should fit snuggly and you can compensate for a loose fitting slide by stuffing some foam or candle wax into it.

As your slide touches the string, keep in mind that you don't need to apply too much pressure to the string: it's more important to keep *consistent* pressure as you slide from note to note. The slide should only cover the string(s) that you are playing slide notes on. For instance, if you are playing notes on the high E-string you should only cover that one string with the slide. A lot of slide playing occurs on the high E-string, and here are a couple points for getting good sound. First, you are covering just the E-string with your slide. As you move from note to note keep consistent pressure on the string. Finally, tilt the slide slightly away from you and the fretboard; thus avoid hitting other strings and nasty overtones.

STRING DAMPENING: A critical aspect of slide playing is string dampening, which can be achieved with both hands. There are times when you want string noise and overtones and there are times when you don't want it. These tips are for those times when you don't want it. First, as you drag the slide along the strings use one or more of the fingers of your left hand to touch and drag along that string with the slide. I use my index finger, which results in a slight 'cupping' of my hand. This technique will rid you of some unsound string overtones. The cupping of the hand also tends to consolidate your hand, making it feel as if it is one appendage moving rather than five independent digits. Also, in conjunction with your thumb planted behind the neck, it helps you to get more of a 'swirling' rotation of your wrist as you move from note to note.

You can also use the palm of your right hand (forgive me, lefties!) to dampen notes. I often rest the palm of my right hand on the bass strings if I am playing slide notes on the higher strings. After I play the note on, for instance, the G-string and slide, then move to the B-string, my palm would descend to the G-string to deaden that string.

In a short but explosive career, Duane Allman (above) set the standard for slide guitar in a rock context. Ben Harper (opposite top) combines soul, funk, and blues with true songwriting craftsmanship. Muddy Waters (opposite below) came to define the

Slide Guitar

THE MUSIC

Introductory exercises

This first group of exercises is intended to get you familiar with using the slide. You will learn some techniques for getting a good sound and become familiar with open G tuning – a tuning that is commonly used in both blues and rock. You will also be introduced to a dominant seventh scale and learn some licks using that scale over a 12-bar blues pattern. In addition, we will cover a simple rhythm pattern for playing a 12-bar blues in open G and fill out the entire 12 bars with licks that you can use whenever you play this progression. You should master these exercises before you move on to any other part of the book.

The exercises are notated in standard notation and tablature (tab). In tab, each line represents a string. The bottom line is the sixth string (low E in standard tuning) and the top line is the first. The numbers on the lines indicate the fret at which you should hold down that string. A sloping line between two notes indicates a slide or 'glissando,' either up or down. A curved line above two notes, with an 'H' above, indicates a hammer-on. Tablature does not include any indication of rhythm. That is supplied by the traditional notation.

In the accompanying explanations, the roman numeral system is sometimes used to identify chords. In any given scale, the chord built on the root note of the scale is I, the chord built on the fourth note is IV, the chord built on the fifth is V, and so on. Lower case numbers – ii, iii, vi, etc – indicate that the chord is minor. In C major, for instance, I = C, ii = Dm, iii = Em, IV = F, V = G, vi = Am.

Before we get started I want you to try a little experiment. Using your finger, fret any place you want on the guitar neck and play a note. Now, move your finger anywhere between that fret and the next one down. You will notice that with a finger fretting the note you can only get one note. Now play the same note (or any other) with your slide, moving the slide up and down over the space between the two frets. You should be able to get three or four distinct notes. These are called 'microtones,' and are pitched in between the normal notes sounded by the frets, which are a semitone apart. Now you can see why proper intonation is so important in slide playing.

Exercise 1

Our first exercise is in open G tuning: DGDGBD, low to high. To get there from standard tuning, tune the sixth string (low E) down two half-steps to D; tune the fifth string (A) down two half-steps to G. You can leave the fourth, third, and second strings alone. Finally, tune the first string (E) down two half-steps to D. In this first exercise you will be practicing moving the slide from note to note. Position the slide directly over the fret, not in between frets as you would normally do if you were fretting the note with your fingers. These are notes from the dominant seventh scale; they provide a good basis for soloing over blues progressions. The slide should only cover the string(s) you are playing, in this case the high E (first) string. You only want to put enough pressure on the string to make the note sound – pressing too hard will lead to string noise. (You will find that a lot of slide playing technique involves avoiding 'bad' sounds like string noise, banging the frets, overtones, etc.)

Exercise 2

Using the same scale as in exercise one, try sliding between the notes of the scale. You will pick the first note and slide to the second. Then you will pick the note you slid to and slide to the next note in the scale. You will be ascending and descending the scale. Notice how your slide sound differs when you descend the scale. Try to keep it consistent with the sound you get when you ascend. The thumb should be securely behind the neck, providing you with the stability that the lack of pressure from your slide is providing on the front of the neck. Try to let the slide 'glide,' keeping very slight yet even pressure as you slide from note to note.

EXERCISE 1 CD track 1

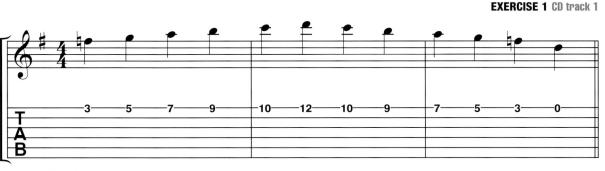

G Tuning

EXERCISE 2 CD track 2

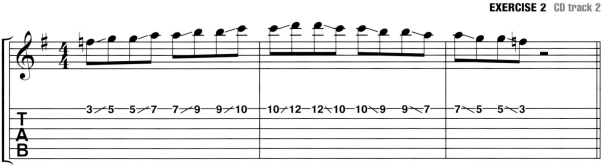

G Tuning

Exercise 3

I have laid out a blues scale in the first position for all six strings. Try to let your slide only cover the strings you are playing. When you start to play the strings beyond the high E-string it is sometimes useful to angle your slide away from the higher strings. If you are playing several strings at once you can, of course, cover more than one string.

Exercise 4

Now let's start playing some licks! As you play this exercise, pay close attention to string damping. Your left-hand index finger should glide along 'behind' the slide. I achieve this by 'cupping' my left hand. You will need to lift the slide off to play the open string in the third beat of this exercise. As you place the slide back down on the string, the index finger touches at precisely the same time to eliminate any unwanted string noise.

EXERCISE 3 CD track 3

G Tuning

EXERCISE 4 CD track 4

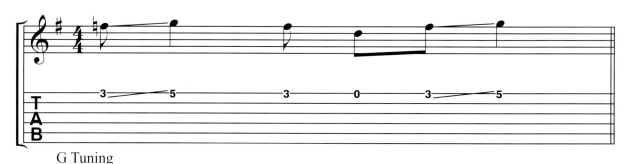

G Tuning

Exercise 5

This is a 'response' to the 'call' made in exercise four. Angle the slide outwards from the fretboard/yourself as you play the lick on the first string; then, as you cover the next three strings, allow the slide to 'flatten' out and cover those strings.

Exercise 6

Here we get to do some sliding backwards using the G-string. In G tuning it is useful to get as much mileage as you can from the G-string, since any time you strike an open G note you are almost certainly hitting the 'right' note.

EXERCISE 5 CD track 5

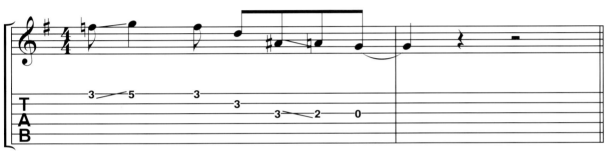

G Tuning

EXERCISE 6 CD track 6

G Tuning

Exercise 7

Let's practice getting some more 'slide mileage' out of every picked note. In this exercise you will pick the first note of each triplet, allowing the slide to do the rest of the work for the following two notes of the triplet. For example, in the first triplet you will pick the third fret then slide all the way up to the seventh fret then back down to the fifth, without lifting the slide. This will take a little work to get it to sound smooth. Remember, try to keep even pressure between each note.

Exercise 8

Before we go any further I want to introduce you to your friend: the 12-bar shuffle rhythm. Many of you probably already know this in standard tuning, but here it is in G tuning – and it's actually easier to play: you don't have to stretch your fingers as much. This rhythm will be the background for the licks we are currently working on. I will complete the 12-bar slide section shortly, but let's get familiar with the rhythm first. If you can record yourself playing this rhythm, all the better – I have also provided a backing track on the CD.

The shuffle rhythm should be played with the right hand damping the strings; this gives you a nice percussive attack. Anchoring the palm of your hand on the bridge of the guitar, experiment with bringing the palm into contact with the strings. As you play you will notice that you have to strike the strings harder to get the strings to sound. This is good. You want a forceful attack. The ideal is not to cut off the sound entirely but to get a sound that lacks the ringing quality of sustained notes while allowing the strings to sound the note(s) you are playing. This technique also proves useful for muting unwanted string noise while you are playing slide.

EXERCISE 7 CD track 7

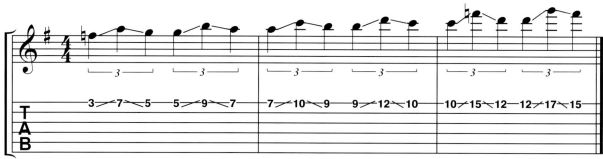

G Tuning

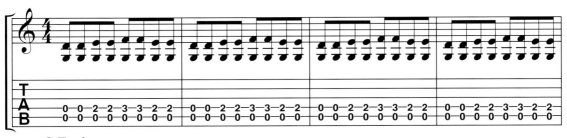

G Tuning

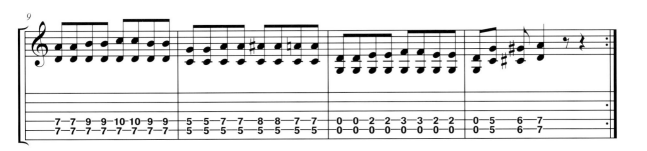

Exercise 9

Here is an entire 12-bar riff you can try out your new slide skills on. There is nothing new in the first four bars, but in the next two bars we do a double-string riff over the C chord at the fifth fret. If you are using a pick I would suggest using all downstrokes through this passage (fingerpickers use your thumb). In measures seven and eight we return to the G chord. These long sustained notes are an opportunity to practice your slide vibrato. To get a good vibrato, you want to make sure that your left-hand thumb is firmly placed behind the neck. You will slide up to the note and once you have arrived you can vibrato by moving the slide back and forth from the note. Make sure you do not go beyond (ie, higher than) the note. In measure nine we follow the V chord (D) with a simple lick at the seventh fret; and in measure ten we do the same thing for the IV chord at the fifth fret. In measure 11 we play the beginning of a simple turnaround with a descending bass line against a constant G note that leads us into an ascending double-string riff back up to D.

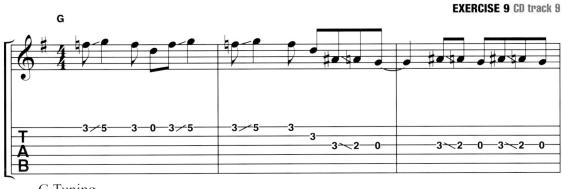

G Tuning

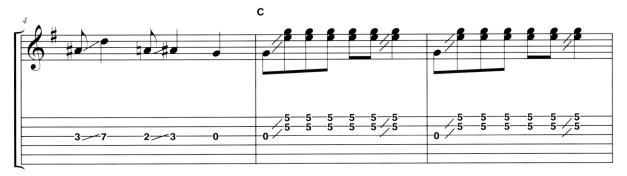

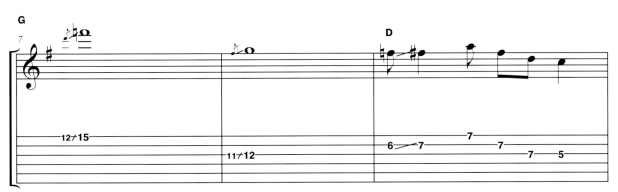

Adding the bass

For the acoustic blues musician, much of the excitement of playing slide is accompanying yourself with a steady bass. If you want to stick to strictly electric slide playing you can skip this section and move forward to the section on rock and electric blues. (Actually, you might want to skip ahead to chapter three to learn some licks and get some practice in D tuning first.) Players who used an alternating bass in open G tuning include Son House, Leo Kottke, Charlie Patton, Black Ace and Robert Johnson. (Often the early recordings are at a different pitch. For instance, Robert Johnson's 'Come on in My Kitchen' was played in G tuning but is heard in A♭, either because of the inadequacies of early recording or because Johnson was not tuned to concert pitch – they didn't have electronic tuners around back then!)

In this chapter try playing the bass notes with your thumb. The melody notes can be played with many combinations of fingers. Many blues players used their thumb, index and middle fingers; some only used thumb and index; and a few used thumb and three fingers. I use the latter method; employing my thumb for the three low bass strings, my index finger for the third (G) string, middle finger for the second (B) string and the ring finger for the first (E) string. The 'four finger' method gives you the most latitude for playing more complicated styles (as with Kottke), but if you want to stick with strictly blues you can often get away with two or three fingers.

Exercise 10

If you have never played a consistent bass with accompanied melody, here is a good place to start. We begin by playing a riff followed by two bass notes. Musically speaking, the riff occupies the first two beats of the measure and the bass, which falls on the downbeat, occupies the last two beats. This is a common technique employed by many blues musicians. The first musical statement could be either a vocal line or instrumental melodic phrase; then the rhythm comes in to propel the song forward (listen to Robert Johnson, in particular, to experience this method).

EXERCISE 10 CD track 10

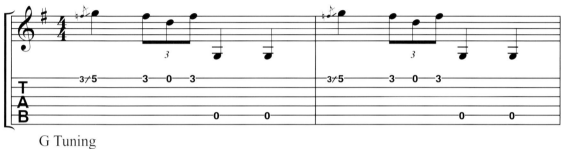

G Tuning

Exercise 11

Note that in G tuning the root bass note is usually on the fifth string, which is tuned to D. In this exercise we travel to the IV chord (C) in our I-IV-V pattern. The chord here is played with the slide covering all the strings. The fifth-string bass note should be played with your thumb, and the third and second strings should be played with index and middle fingers respectively. This a good exercise for getting used to playing bass and melody notes at the same time. This method, called a 'pinch,' will be used significantly in the following exercises.

EXERCISE 11 CD track 11

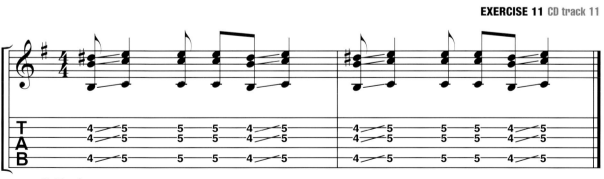

G Tuning

Exercise 12

Here we return to the I chord for a high melody riff and our two-note bass response. In the first exercise we used one and then two strings for our melody notes. In this exercise you will have to travel between three strings for the melody. This will be a good opportunity for you to practice using different fingers for different strings. If you decide to go the index/middle finger route, think of using them in pairs: if you are playing melody notes on the first and second strings plant your middle and index accordingly; then, when the third string comes in, simply shift your index finger up to the third string.

EXERCISE 12 CD track 12

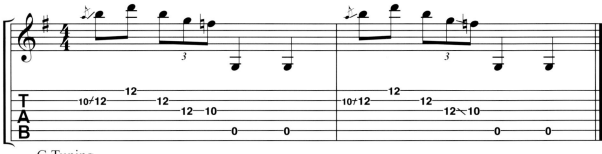

G Tuning

Exercise 13

In this exercise you will be combining the last two exercises to play the first eight bars of a 12-bar blues. Notice that you will move from the first position/open to the fifth fret for the C chord and then up to the 12th fret for a higher register riff in G. Practice this move slowly and in time. (Note: it is useful to use a metronome to keep you on the beat. In the beginning set your metronome to 80bpm, then work up to 120bpm, making sure that the bass notes fall on the downbeat.)

EXERCISE 13 CD track 13

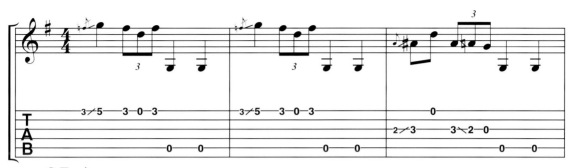

G Tuning

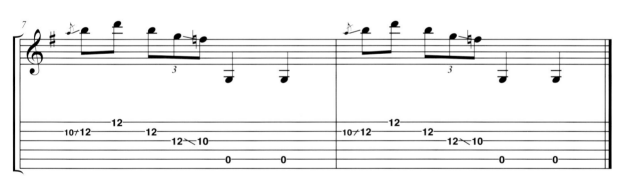

Exercise 14

We finish up our 12-bar blues in G with a move to the V chord in the ninth measure. The first two beats are played at the seventh fret, just like we did for the IV chord (fifth fret), but then we play a little melodic phrase around the same position (basically playing an arpeggiated version of the chord). Same thing for the IV chord return at the tenth measure/fifth fret. Then we have a turnaround in the 11th measure that should be played with your left hand fingers (not the slide). For the right hand in this turnaround you will be playing thumb, pinch (thumb-index), thumb, pinch…

EXERCISE 14 CD track 14

G Tuning

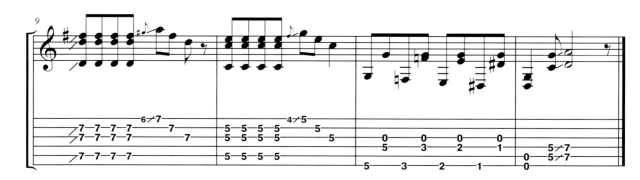

Exercise 15

Let's move on to playing a consistent bass. Playing with the thumb, the bass now falls on every downbeat: boom-boom-boom-boom. At the beginning of each measure you will also play a pinched melody note on the first beat with your finger (ring or middle).

EXERCISE 15 CD track 15

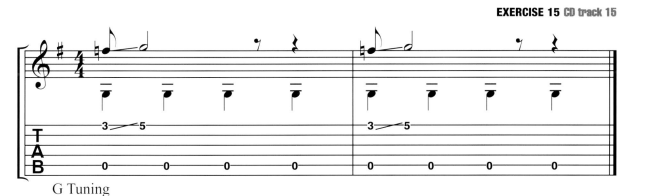

G Tuning

Exercise 16

Again you will be playing a consistent bass and a pinched melody note on the first beat of each measure, but you will also be playing a melody note between the second and third beat, ie, on the 'and' or upbeat. This is probably the trickiest maneuver you will have to master for fingerpicking blues. Many times students have difficulty separating the bass from the finger and there is a tendency for the thumb to want to follow the fingers. TAKE IT SLOW! Try just playing the melody with your metronome so that you get the feel for where the melody lands in the four-beat sequence. Then add the bass and TAKE IT SLOW! Sometimes, if I am having a particularly tough time with a passage I will break it down to just two beats. Then I will 'back out' and play four beats and so on until I have worked the difficult passage into the context of the whole. Oh, by the way, TAKE IT SLOW!

EXERCISE 16 CD track 16

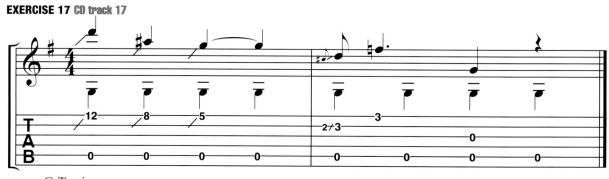

G Tuning

Exercise 17

This exercise simply adds more melody notes and, in the second measure, makes you bring in the second string with the first.

EXERCISE 17 CD track 17

G Tuning

Exercise 18

Often, in fingerpicked blues, the bass travels between two or more strings instead of a 'monotonic' single string bass. For this exercise I want you to put the slide down and just focus on playing the piece with your fingers. Your thumb will be alternating between the fifth and fourth string: boom-chuck, boom-chuck. Practice this piece just going through the bass part at first. It is a standard 12-bar blues in G. All the melody notes are played on the first string. When you get to the fifth measure you will have to barre the fret from the fifth string down.

EXERCISE 18 CD track 18

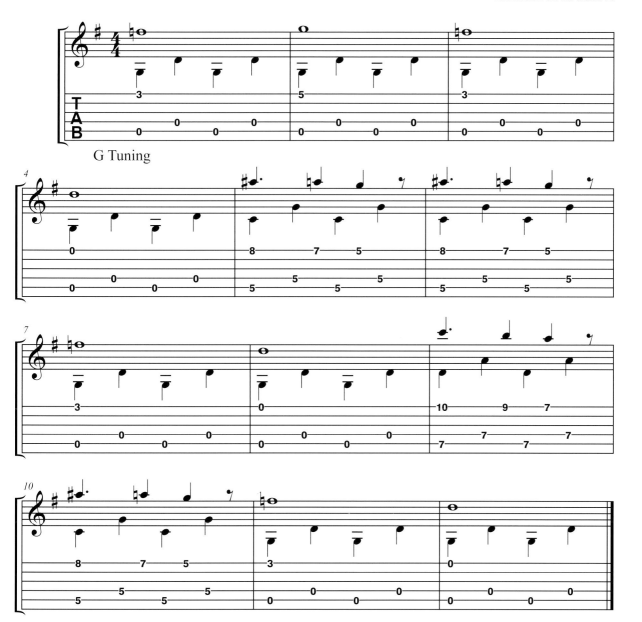

G Tuning

Exercise 19

When you are feeling comfortable with all of the above exercises you will be ready to tackle this challenging piece, another 12-bar blues in G. You won't be using a slide here. Rather, I want you to get comfortable with the bass pattern, as it is a little more complex than what we have been doing. The benefit of playing an alternating bass in G tuning is that you can get a nice 'bouncing' feeling by alternating between the fifth and fourth *and* the sixth and fourth strings. Check out the bass for the I (G) chord in this exercise. The bass should be played: fifth string, fourth string, sixth string, fourth string... as a repetitive pattern. I have also introduced a new chord substitution for the IV and V chords. The C7 chord looks like a first position C chord, but the altered tuning yields a seventh. This is a great sounding chord! The bass pattern for the IV and V chords (C7 and D7) is simplified to being a repetitive fifth string, fourth string combination.

EXERCISE 19 CD track 19

G Tuning

D tuning: basics

The other major blues open tuning is D tuning (DADF#AD), sometimes called Vestapol tuning. Open E tuning (EBEG#BE) is another version of this tuning: the relationship of the strings to each other is the same, but open E is higher pitched than open D. To get to open D from standard tuning: tune your low E (sixth) string down two half-steps to D, your third string from G down half a step to F#, your second string down two half-steps to A, and your first string down two half-steps from E to D. The fifth and fourth strings stay on A and D respectively.

One of the benefits of open D is that you get three strings tuned to D; this can give the music a 'droning' quality as you apply finger-picking techniques. You also get a high melody string (first) that has the root note available in the open position – as opposed to open G, where you don't reach the root note until the fifth fret on the first string.

Exercise 20

Many of the exercises in this section will use a dominant seventh scale. Here the scale is laid out in linear fashion on the first string.

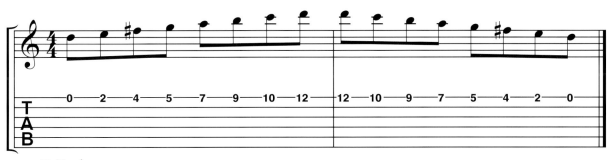

D Tuning

Exercise 21

The other scale we will use is a minor pentatonic (blues scale). The riffs we will be working on throughout this book are mainly derived from the pentatonic and seven-note scales. I have laid out the pentatonic scale on all six strings.

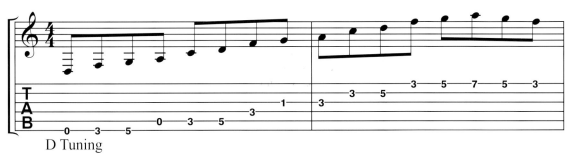

D Tuning

Exercise 22

Here you will get a taste of using the open first D-string to get some cool licks. The triplet feel starts out with a double open note then culminates with the slide note moving up the scale I introduced in exercise 1B. This lick sounds best when played fast.

EXERCISE 22 CD track 22

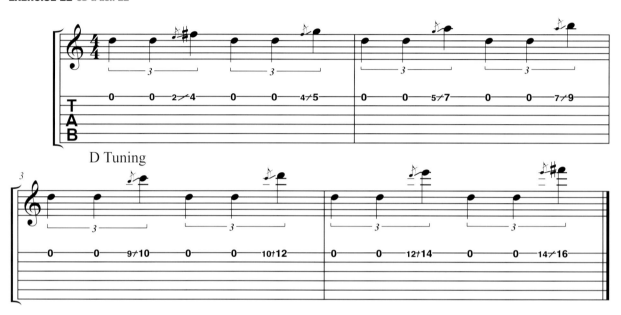

D Tuning

Exercise 23

Let's get some more practice sliding back and forth between notes. We start at the high end of the dominant seventh scale. In measure one, pick the first note of the triplet at the tenth fret, then slide to the 12th and back to the tenth without picking the note again. The sustain of slide notes can give us some extended melodies without picking each note. This can be pretty evocative, especially as the notes decay yet the slide continues: it's what I call the 'drunken sailor' effect. In the final measure, instead of playing slide you will do a simple hammer-on and pull-off: same picking as all the previous triplets.

EXERCISE 23 CD track 23

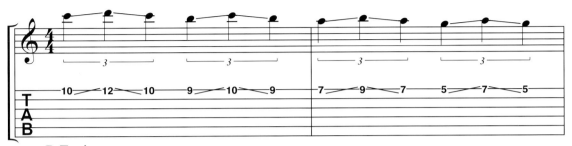

D Tuning

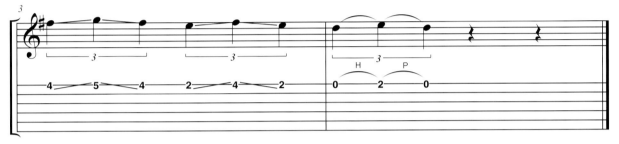

Exercise 24

Let's try this technique in a two bar lick. Start off with a hammer-on (indicated by H) on the second string and then play an open note on the first string. You can either flatpick or fingerpick this exercise. If you fingerpick, use two fingers on your right hand to play this opening lick: either thumb and index or whichever two fingers you would normally use for finger-picking the second and first string. When you get to the slide lick you will only pick once but play six notes! This will test your accuracy and ability to keep the slide on the string without lifting, keeping even pressure. The last note of the lick should be picked.

EXERCISE 24 CD track 24

D Tuning

Exercise 25

This exercise has a bit of a gospel flavor. It starts out with lick similar to the previous exercise (indicated by H), then goes right to the IV chord for a strummed chord that we slide into. Pay attention to the V chord in the fourth measure: you will be seeing more of this one down the line. The exercise finishes up with a chord run: ii-IV-V. Play this exercise slowly and freely; sound is more important than tempo.

Exercises 26 and 27

Here are two simple rhythm exercises for playing a 12-bar shuffle in D tuning. You should be familiar with these. In fact, if you have the capability you should record yourself playing these rhythms and practice your slide licks over the recorded version. This achieves two things: it gives you background for slide and other licks and it makes your rhythm more solid.

D Tuning

EXERCISE 26 CD track 26

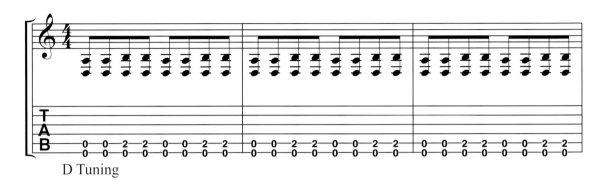

D Tuning

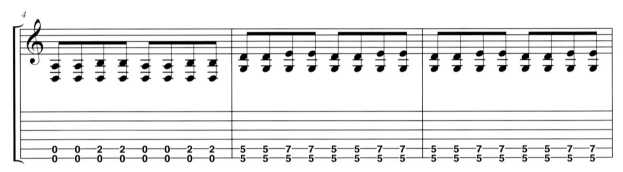

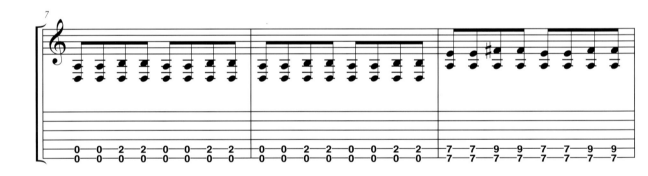

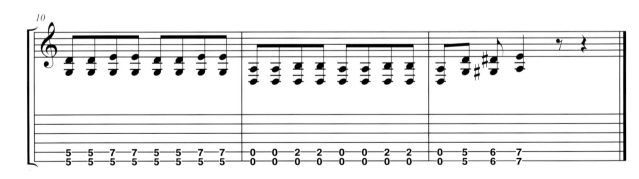

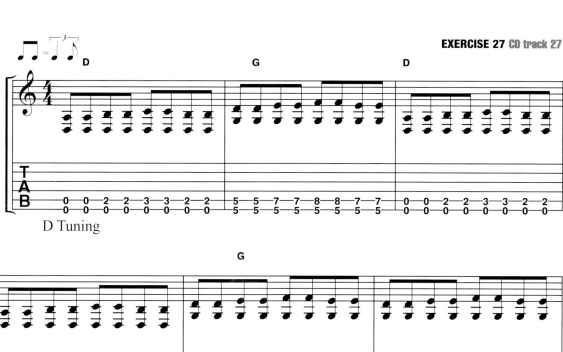

D Tuning

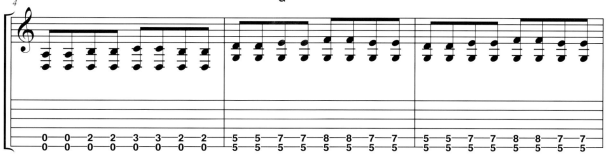

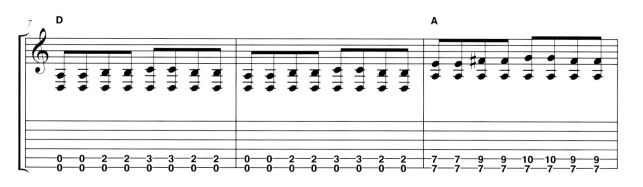

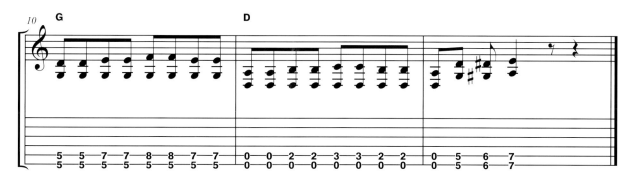

Exercise 28

Okay, here it is: the slide riff that everybody should know! This is a variation on Robert Johnson's 'Dust My Broom.' It can be played strumming style or fingerpicked style. The key to this riff is the flow from the triplet riff in the first measure to the shuffle rhythm in the second measure. The fact is the shuffle is really a triplet with the second note missing. Thus you get Da daDa daDa da… where Da (with a capital D) represents the downbeat.

If you are using a flat pick the triplet should be picked/strummed:

down/up/down   **up/down/up**   **down/up/down**

If you are finger picking you should try:

thumb/index/thumb   **index/thumb/index**   **thumb/index/thumb**

You are effectively strumming up/down consistently but the emphasis is on the downbeat, which occurs in different places – as far as your strum is concerned – because of the triplet rhythm. The second measure is all downstrokes played with the thumb.

   This lick is worth working out really well. Think of yourself at the crossroads on a dark summer night, the cicadas humming in your ear, the sheriff on your trail. A stranger approaches and offers you a drink from a mysterious bottle… You will be a big hit at parties!

EXERCISE 28 CD track 28

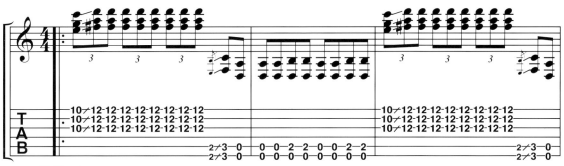

D Tuning

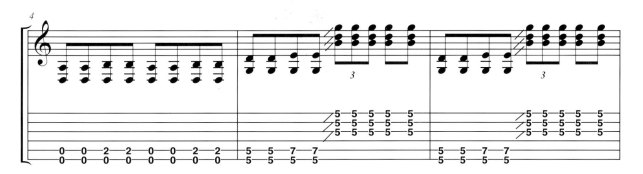

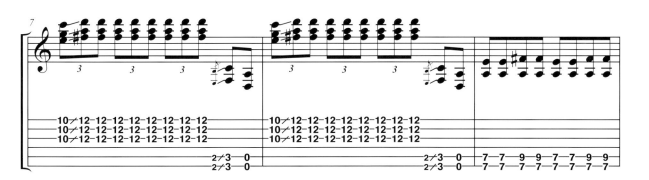

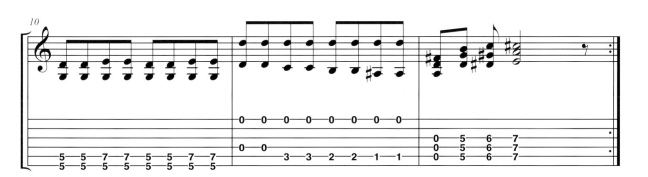

Adding the bass in D tuning

I love playing acoustic fingerstyle blues in open D tuning. The alternating bass between the sixth and fourth strings gives a nice drive and bounce to the music. As I mentioned before, the first string is great for open string licks and, well, it's the first open tuning I learned – like your first love, it holds a special place in your heart.

Exercise 29

We are going to use a monotonic bass for this first exercise. The single string bass has a more 'menacing' sound than the alternating bass. The bass is played with the thumb and should be muted by using the palm damping technique. You can experiment with how much damping to use by placing the palm of your right hand on the bridge of your guitar then 'rolling' it over onto the strings. Obviously, the more you press the more the damping effect. Instead of the dominant seventh scales I used in the opening exercises of the previous chapter, I am using our old friend the minor pentatonic. Note: the minor third is played at the third fret of the first string in open D tuning: this is the primary note that defines the minor scale(s). The use of a minor pentatonic with a monotonic bass (instead of an alternating bass) lends this exercise a 'darker,' more ominous sound. Notice that the exercise starts off with a single-string melody slide, then proceeds to add a string to the melody in the following three measures. This gives more urgency and propels the music forward.

Exercise 30

This exercise has a similar feel to the previous exercise, but uses a higher register for the melody. I think the toughest part of this exercise is keeping the bass consistent as you play the melody notes between the beat. Keep aware of the tendency of the thumb to follow the fingers. You want to keep them separate. The thumb is your time keeper and your melody operates independently. The IV and V chords (fifth and seventh fret respectively) are played with the slide covering all the strings.

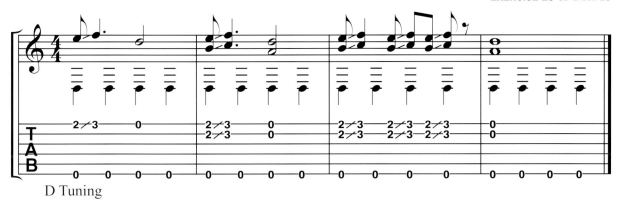

D Tuning

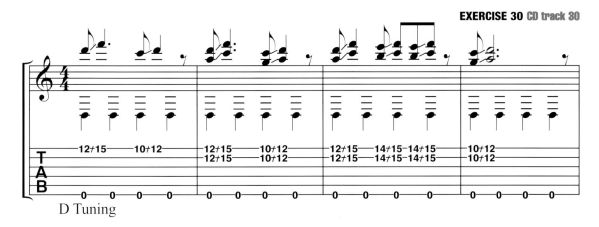

D Tuning

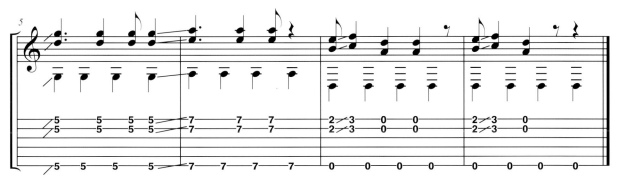

Exercise 31

Let's move into playing an alternating bass. Your thumb will alternate bass notes between the sixth and fourth strings. You will notice that the alternating bass makes the music 'bounce.' Whereas the monotonic bass pumps the music, driving it forward like a late model Chrysler down a two-lane highway, the alternating bass bounces like a ride in a hay-wagon. The right-hand pattern is the same in each measure.

1	and	2	and	3	and	4	and
Bass		bass		bass		bass	
Melody			melody		melody		

Exercise 32

Here is a nice slow-throbbing monotonic shuffle bass song. Play it slow and 'greasy.' It has a very cool turnaround to start off. This opening sequence is based around eighth-note triplets with the middle triplet missing in the bass – this is in fact what goes on when you play a shuffle rhythm. In measure three the bass is notated as straight eighth-notes but it is actually the same feel as the bass in the first three beats of measure one. In measure nine you will be playing the melody with your slide and alternating with fretted and open notes. More triplets in measure ten: I would play these with thumb and two fingers of the right hand. I like the 'new' turnaround in measure 13 – it has a 'creepy' feel.

EXERCISE 31 CD track 31

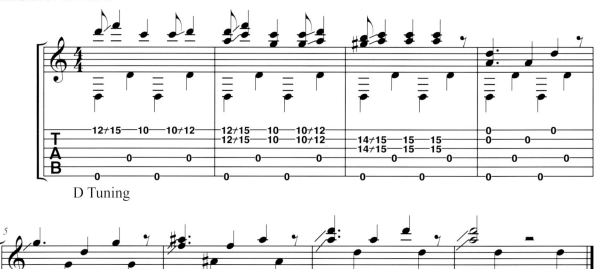

D Tuning

D Tuning

EXERCISE 32 CD track 32

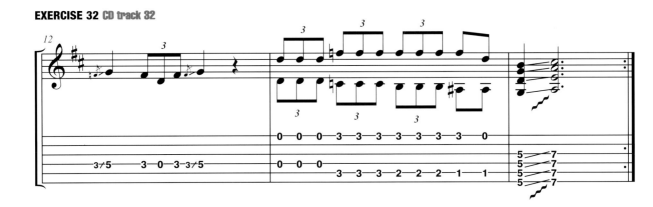

'Hope Springs Eternal'

I call this one 'Hope Springs Eternal.' It should be played fast! The right hand pattern is the same as the previous exercise. Coordinating the hammer-on to slide lick in measure one-two is the crux of this tune. There are some melody notes that reach pretty far up the neck in measure six, but even if you have a short scale neck you should be able to reach these. (Note: a nice part of slide playing is that you can reach notes beyond the length of your fretboard.) Your entire hand follows the slide and the palm becomes your string damping device instead of the tip of your index finger. Try sliding beyond the 19th fret to the sound hole/pickups and you'll see what I mean. Rod Price from Foghat used this trick very effectively.

The trickiest part of this exercise is the passage in measures 9-11. I start off the first beat using the slide, then remove the slide to play the open notes in the second beat. Then I forgo the slide and use my thumb to cover the sixth string and first finger to barre strings one to four in beats three and four. In the next measure, I keep the same hand position letting the third finger play the bent note at the seventh fret. Left hand releases in the fourth beat and the slide barres again for the chords in measure 11. Whew! It's not as hard as it sounds.

HOPE SPRINGS ETERNAL CD track 33

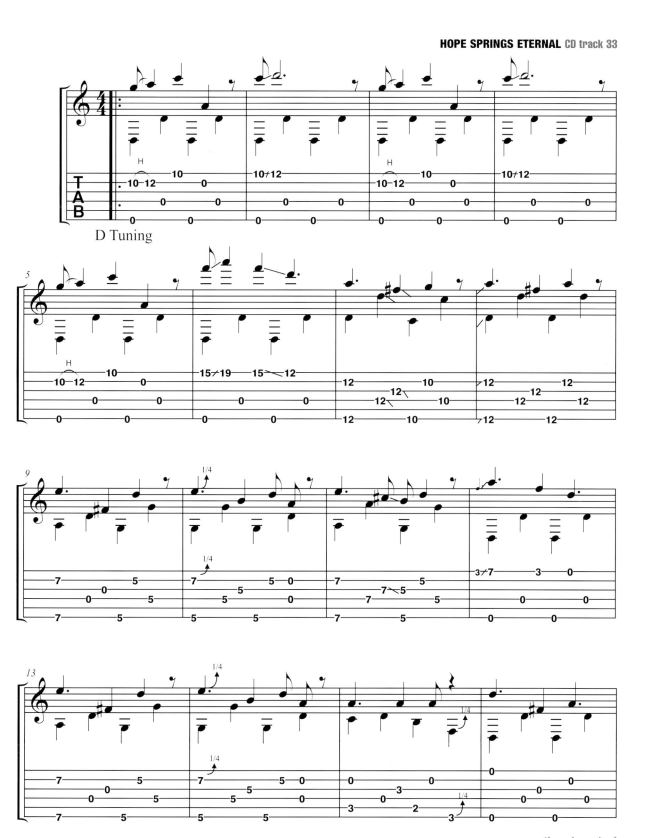

D Tuning

continued overleaf

HOPE SPRINGS ETERNAL *continued*

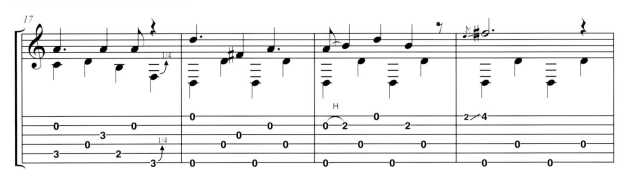

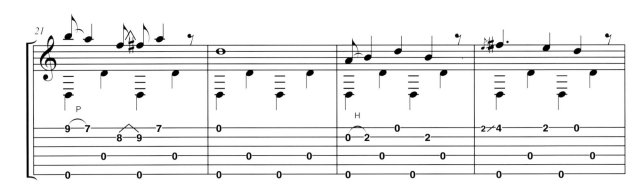

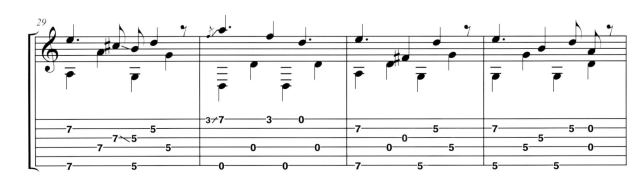

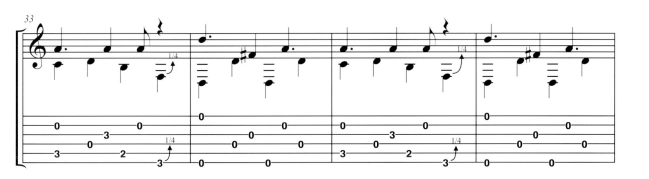

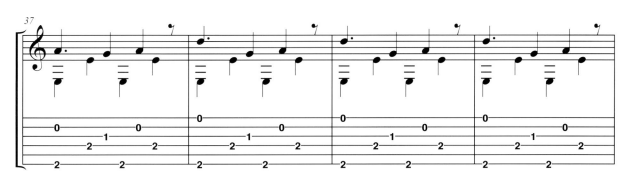

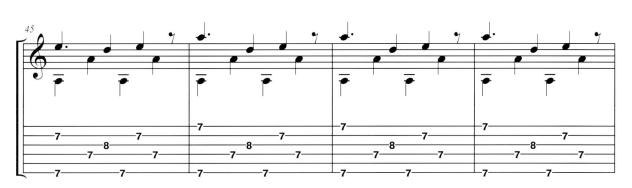

continued overleaf

HOPE SPRINGS ETERNAL *continued*

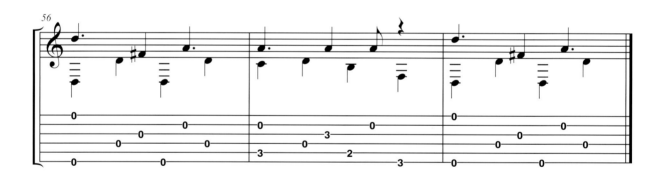

Early blues

In this chapter we will be playing exercises in the style of venerable blues artists such as Robert Johnson, Charlie Patton, Son House, Blind Willie Johnson and Tampa Red. Much of this playing involves using an alternating or constant bass, so you should review the preceding chapters in order to feel comfortable playing these songs. We will be working in both G and D tunings, as well as introducing two new tunings: D minor, otherwise known as DADFAD, a very close cousin of open D tuning; and dropped D tuning (see below).

OPEN G TUNING SONGS:

'Son House Groove'

This exercise is very reminiscent of Son House's playing. It's in open G: DGDGBD. Son House's arrangements have very few chord changes. In fact, in this piece, there is no discernable chord change. Instead, Son would mix it up with different rhythmic flourishes and dynamic string popping, to give the music the illusion of movement. The opening motif is repeated throughout. In measure five what you are playing is still a G chord (even though it looks like the upper register of a minor triad). This passage kicks up the rhythmic drive of the piece by laying out a triplet then falling into a shuffle type rhythm. The last eighth-note of measure six plops you right back down into the original groove. Measures nine and ten are a classic House device, a descending octave run played on the sixth and fourth strings. The idea is to 'pop' the sixth string by getting your thumb underneath the string and 'plang!'

'Crossroads Groove'

Another G tuning song, this one is very similar to Robert Johnson's 'Crossroads.' The first five measures are an introduction, with the fourth measure being a popular Johnson turnaround. In measure ten you will be playing a C chord with a slight melodic riff and a rhythmic signature much like what we played in the previous exercise (measure five of 'Son House Groove'). Johnson's playing was amazingly diverse. He didn't really play solos, but he would interject riffs and rhythmic jabs that made it sound like he was playing a lot more than he actually was. He was an expert at alluding to a bass line or chord without playing the full accompaniment.

SON HOUSE GROOVE CD track 34

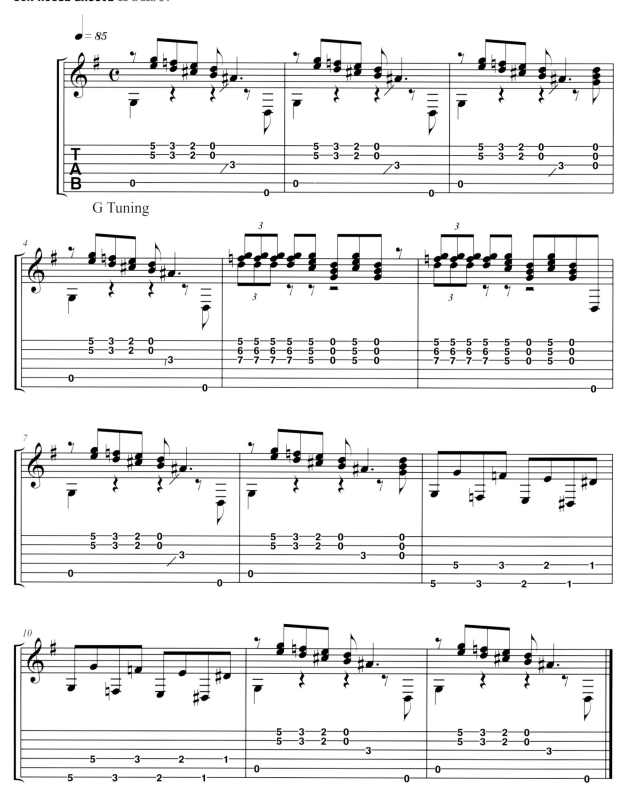

CROSSROADS GROOVE CD track 35

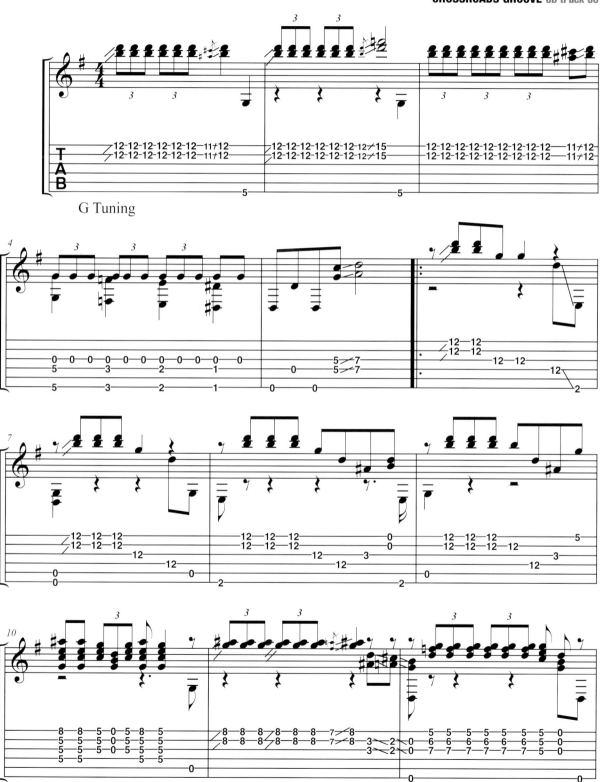

G Tuning

continued overleaf

CROSSROADS GROOVE *continued*

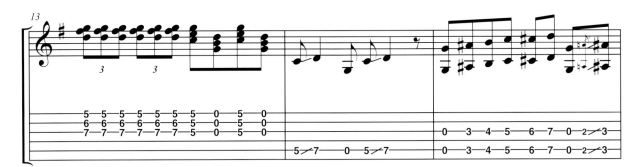

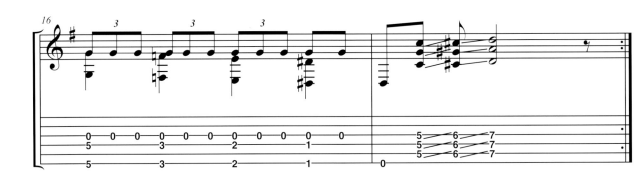

'Poor Man Blues'

This tune is modeled after Gus Cannon's rendition of 'Poor Boy Long Ways from Home,' the oldest known bottleneck tune on record. Gus was the leader of Cannon's Jug Stompers, a popular recording ensemble from the 1920s that included banjo, harmonica, and kazoo in addition to a percussive whiskey jug. In this piece you get a feel for the transition of ragtime to blues.

POOR MAN BLUES CD track 36

G Tuning

'Boogie On A Roll'

This is just a fun piece that has the boogie-woogie feel of the era.

BOOGIE ON A ROLL CD track 37

G Tuning

OPEN D SONGS

'Tampa Red Style'

Tampa Red was a prolific blues artist from Chicago. (He was raised in Tampa, but moved to Chicago, where he gained fame for his incredible slide playing.) This piece echoes 'Denver Blues,' one of his better known pieces. It is in D tuning: DADF#AD. The opening has a steady monotonic bass accompanied by triplet melody notes. I really like the way the melody is sometimes set off from the bass in this piece. Instead of the rhythmic flourishes that we heard in the previous two examples, in this example we get melodic flourishes. Measure five has a challenging yet extremely cool chord change to G7. The two bass notes are played with the thumb; simply bear down a little more and you will be able to incorporate the fourth string. The melody has a hammer-on/slide riff which might take a little practice, but once you get this one you'll get asked back to the pub for sure.

TAMPA RED STYLE CD track 38

D Tuning

'Charlie Patton Groove'

Patton's influence can be heard in almost all the old Delta blues men, including Robert Johnson and Son House. This piece alludes to his classic 'Spoonful Blues.' In this one you will spend a lot of time barring all six strings with your slide, with brief respites for single-string playing. It is in open D tuning. Using a slightly different chord pattern from most blues, this one incorporates the ii and vi chords in addition to the standard I IV V.

CHARLIE PATTON GROOVE *CD track 39*

D Tuning

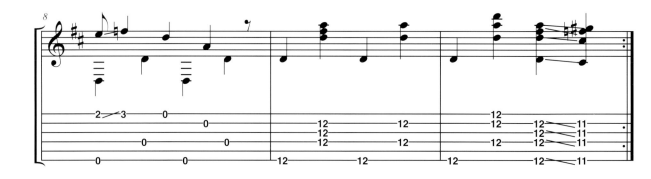

OPEN D MINOR TUNING

'The Forlorn'

Here is a tune in open D minor tuning: DADFAD. To get to open D minor from open D tuning, simply lower the G (3rd) string a half-step from F# to F. This song is based on Blind Willie Johnson's 'Dark is the Night, Cold was the Ground.' Considered one of the greatest gospel performers of his generation, Blind Willie Johnson is thought to have been born in 1900 in Marlin, Texas. He died in the 1940s in Beaumont, Texas. Ry Cooder also recorded an excellent version of this song, and claims that 'Dark is the Night…' was the inspiration for his soundtrack to *Paris, Texas*.

THE FORLORN CD track 40

continued overleaf

THE FORLORN *continued*

DROPPED D TUNING

'Goin' Down to Richmond'

Here is a longer piece based – somewhat – on Ry Cooder's playing. I know what you're thinking: "Hey, Ry Cooder is not an old bluesman." Yes, but much of his playing is derived from old blues, yet has a distinctive Cooder quality about it, so this piece really belongs here. It is in dropped D tuning: DADGBE. To get to this tuning from standard tuning, simply lower the E (6th) string down a whole step to D. The first half of this song is meant to be played without the slide on your finger – some of the phrases can not be played with the slide on. Then, in the second half of the piece, you pick up the slide to play along with the monotonic bass. The opening of the tune has a droning quality meant to evoke a 'swampy' Delta feel. Starting in measure nine, you enter into a pseudo-steady bass section. This section has several four-bar call and response phrases: the first three bars are the call and the fourth measure has a varied response. In measure 25, the bass starts to alternate more. In measure 43 we play some nice harmonics against a sustained bass. Play the bass with your left-hand first finger and play the harmonics with either your pinky or third finger. At the end of this section I usually let the last bass note ring for a measure, allowing me time to put the slide on my pinky for part II.

In part II we are playing a monotonic bass with slide notes. Note that when you go to the IV chord in measure six you should fret the bass with your left-hand index finger while playing the slide. In measure 13 we shift to a very simple fingering for A7 and use an alternating bass. The same holds true for the G7 in measure 18.

GOIN' DOWN TO RICHMOND CD track 41

No Bottleneck

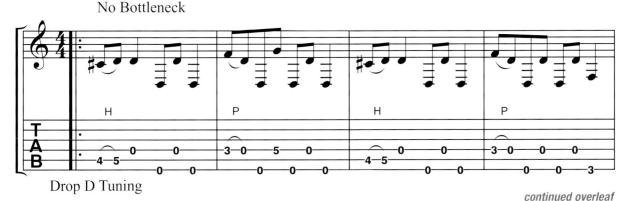

Drop D Tuning

continued overleaf

GOIN' DOWN TO RICHMOND *continued*

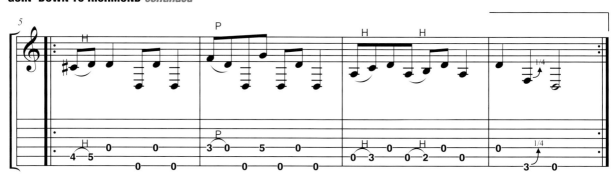

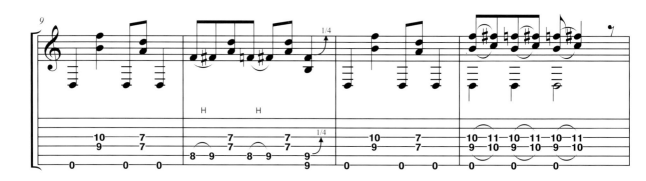

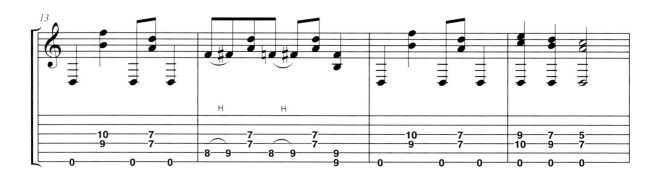

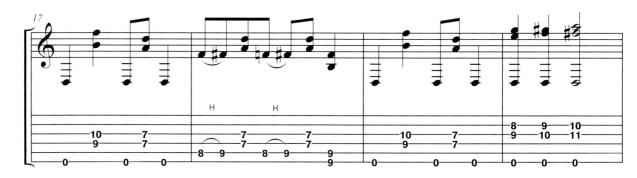

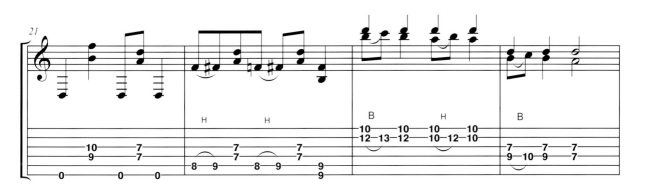

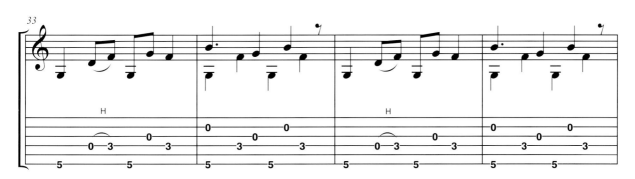

continued overleaf

GOIN' DOWN TO RICHMOND *continued*

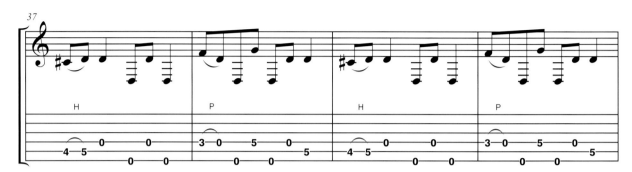

End Part I: place slide on pinky for Part II

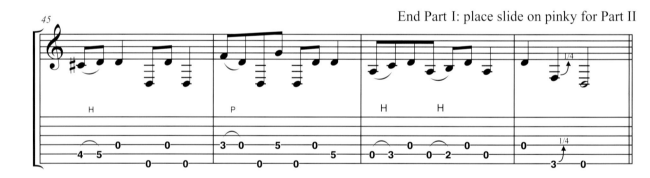

Bottleneck throughout--->

GOIN' DOWN TO RICHMOND PART II

Drop D Tuning

continued overleaf

GOIN' DOWN TO RICHMOND PART II *continued*

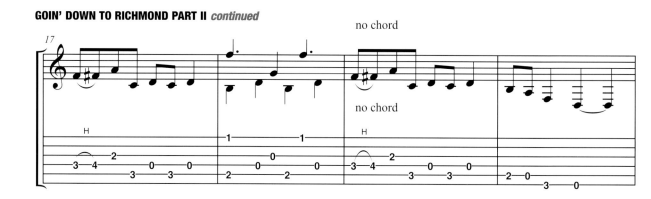

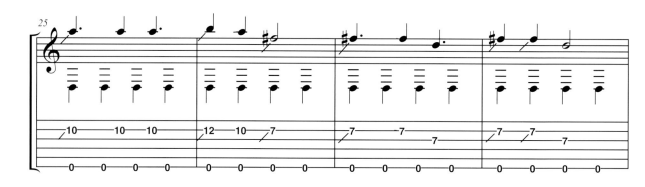

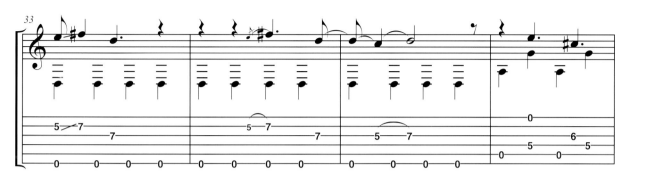

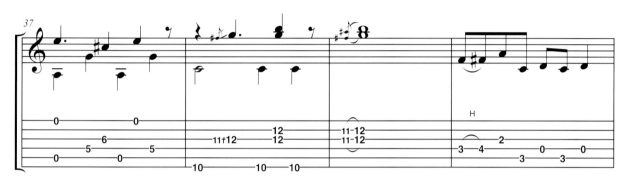

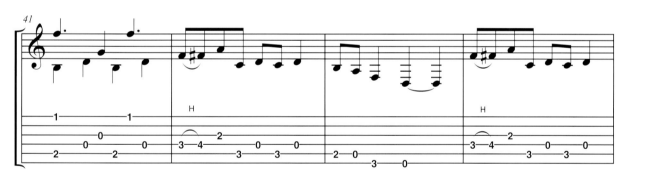

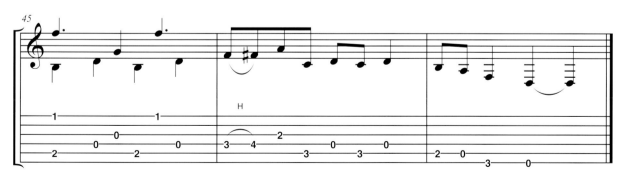

Electric blues and rock

The electric guitar made it possible for slide guitarists to get more sustain from their instruments, so you will find yourself playing fewer notes in the following exercises. Ah, but what notes! The emphasis will be more on articulation and subtleties of vibrato and note duration. As you listen more and more to players, concentrating on their approach to slide, you begin to hear each player's unique style. For example, Duane Allman played with a thin glass slide; you can hear that to get his sound he had to strike the string harder than someone who used, for instance, a heavier slide made of metal or brass.

Equipment

Most of the exercises in this chapter – except where noted – use some kind of distortion or overdrive device. What kind of device you use is entirely up to you – with so many flavors of distortion and pedals on the market it can be a bit daunting. I recommend that you choose something that provides overdrive more than distortion. You want to emulate the sound of an amplifier being turned up and thus being overdriven. The more distortion you add to the mix the more difficult it will be to control string-damping, etc.

Getting a good slide sound on an electric can be difficult, especially since most electric guitarists keep the action of their strings pretty low. If raising the action on your guitar is difficult, try using heavier gauge strings – the tighter tension that heavier strings require can offset some of the fret noise you get with a guitar that has low action.

Tunings

Most of the exercises in this chapter are in standard tuning: EADGBE. Players like George Harrison and Duane Allman preferred standard tuning to open tunings. The advantages to playing in standard tuning are obvious: less time spent tuning and retuning; you don't have to rethink the fretboard. In a band setting, guitarists do not need to hold down the bass or rhythm all the time so they have a freedom that Delta-style players didn't have. The drawback to standard tuning is that some multi-string phrases sound pretty awkward and you have to finesse it a little more.

'Muddy Waters Style'

For this exercise, in G tuning, you can keep the tone pretty clean. Muddy did a lot of slide playing on the bass strings and that's where the emphasis lies. This exercise is mainly pick or right-hand thumb based, but in measure five you start to use some simultaneous bass and melody notes. If you are holding a flat pick you can simply pick the bass notes and use your ring finger to play the melody notes. In this piece you can hear a synthesis of rural and city sounds. There is a little more drive in the music but there is still a hint of the alternating bass and rural 'bounce.'

MUDDY WATERS STYLE CD track 42

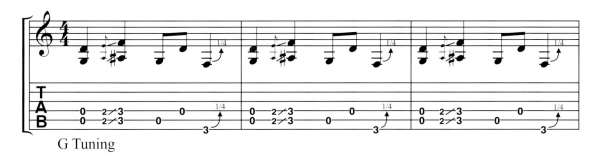

G Tuning

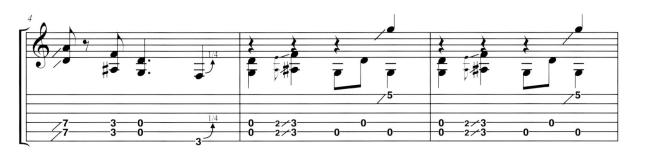

continued overleaf

MUDDY WATERS STYLE *continued*

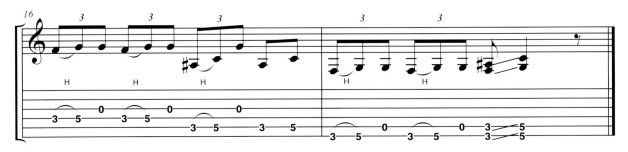

'Statesboro Bros.'

For the Allman Brothers, 'Statesboro Blues' was a staple of their set while Duane Allman was alive. This Blind Willie McTell song provided a perfect opportunity for Duane to strut his slide licks. This piece isn't exactly like 'Statesboro Blues,' but it is very similar. The 12-bar blues is jump-started with an eight-bar intro which features the slide. The emphasis here is on long drawn out slides with occasional snaps of the wrist, like the flicking out of a match. Most of the notes are played on the first and second strings. Allman was unsurpassed for getting great tone; a careful listen to his playing will help you achieve a great slide sound.

STATESBORO BROS. CD track 43

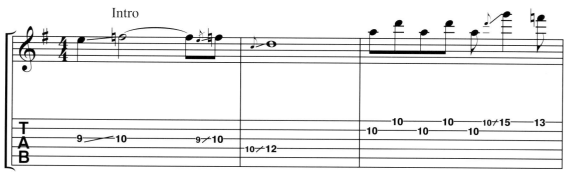

Standard Tuning

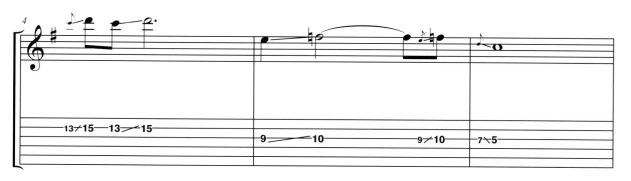

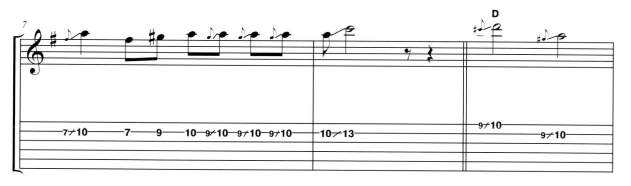

continued overleaf

STATESBORO BROS. *continued*

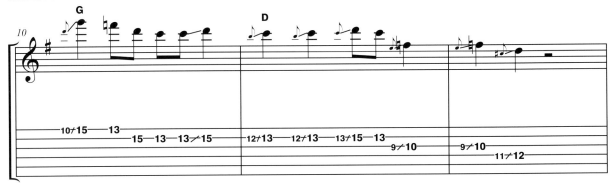

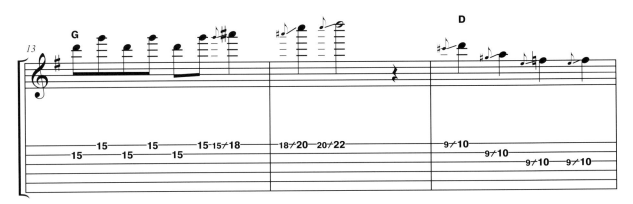

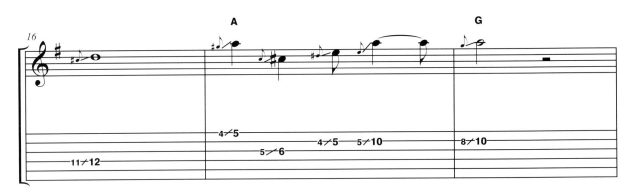

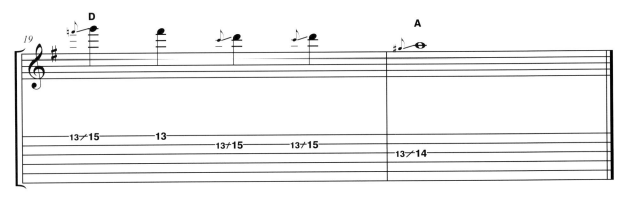

'George Harrison Groove'

George Harrison, like Duane Allman, preferred to play slide in standard tuning. This piece, while not representative of any particular Harrison song, is representative of his approach to playing. The melody is highlighted, with emphasis on playing articulately and gracefully. The backing chords are played with a simple 'down down/up down down' pattern.

GEORGE HARRISON GROOVE CD track 44

Standard Tuning

continued overleaf

GEORGE HARRISON GROOVE *continued*

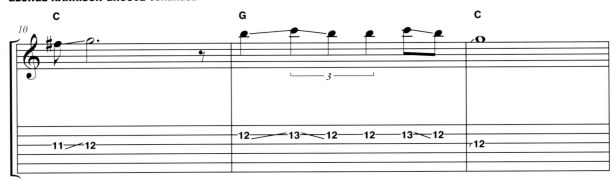

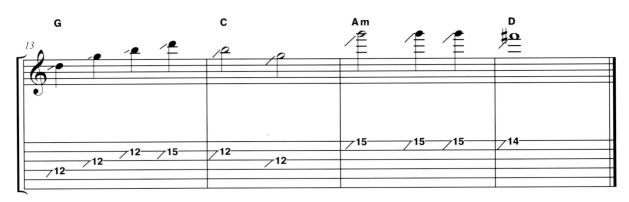

'Lowell George Groove'

Lowell George, the driving force behind the band Little Feat, used his slide prowess to create a slippery swamp groove behind the band's New Orleans-flavored rock sound. His playing was not quite as out-front as Duane Allman's; he chose instead to play in support of the song. Like Muddy Waters, he often emphasized bass runs alongside higher melodic notes. This piece travels between one chord change: A-E and E-A. Remember to stay in the groove, slightly behind the beat. George's playing was funky!

Swampy New Orleans Feel

Standard Tuning

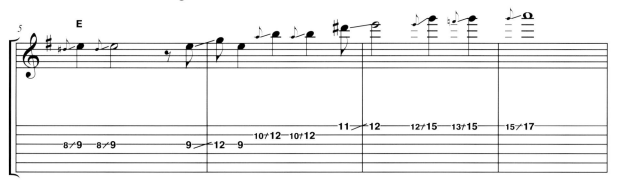

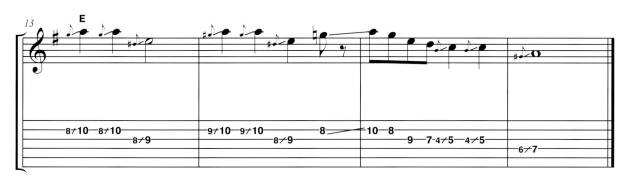

'Sonny Landreth Style'

Sonny Landreth, a sideman for songwriter John Hiatt, is one of those few artists – like Roy Rogers and Duane Allman – known exclusively for his slide playing. In this piece we are back in G tuning. The opening sequence is a Landreth staple. He uses his palm to mute the strings as he strums downward through a series of double-string eighth-notes. The feeling is one of subdued urgency that explodes into a final slide note with lots of vibrato. We then travel to a IV chord rhythm run that should be familiar by now.

SONNY LANDRETH STYLE CD track 46

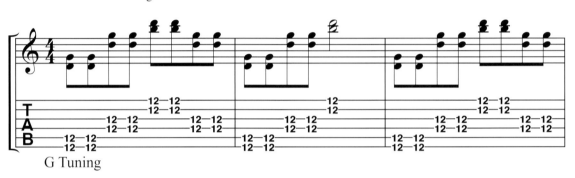

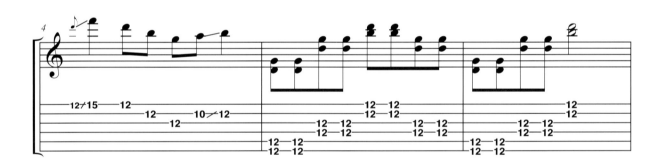

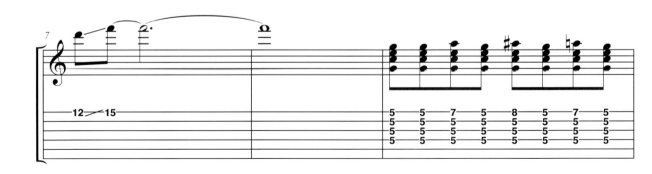

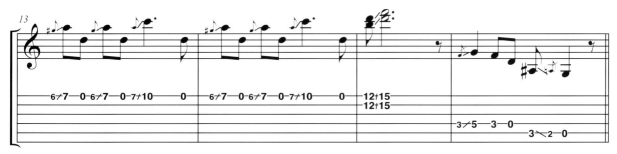

'Sleepwalker'

Every few years a guitar virtuoso like Brian Setzer or Joe Satriani comes along to do a remake of 'Sleepwalk,' the classic Santo and Johnny instrumental. Unfortunately, this is not a song made for virtuosos. The simple haunting quality of the slide melody (played on lap steel) in 'Sleepwalk' is a thing of beauty not to be improved upon. Here is a slightly different version of that song. It is in 3/4 time and follows a classic I-vi-IV-V chord progression. Nothing terribly technically challenging here except the trick in measure 14, which I learned from Bob Brozman. To play a 'Brozman,' you sound the harmonic at the 12th fret on the first string, then place your slide behind the nut before 'rolling' it over the nut and back up the string to play the remaining notes of the phrase. This technique allows the harmonic to sustain and gives the notes a bell-like quality. Use open C tuning (CGCGCE, low to high).

SLEEPWALKER CD track 47

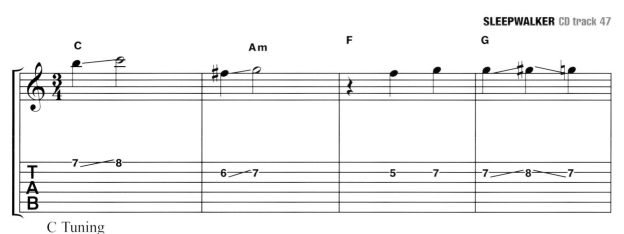

C Tuning

continued overleaf

SLEEPWALKER *continued*

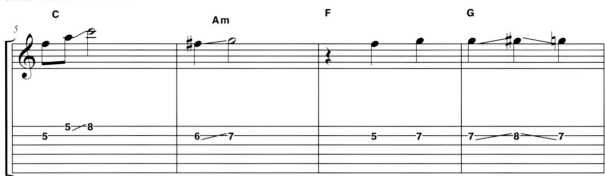

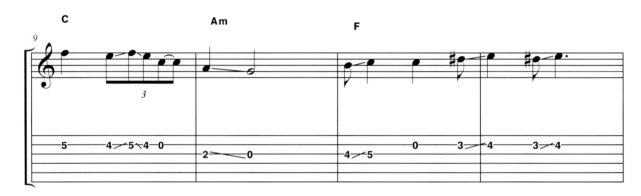

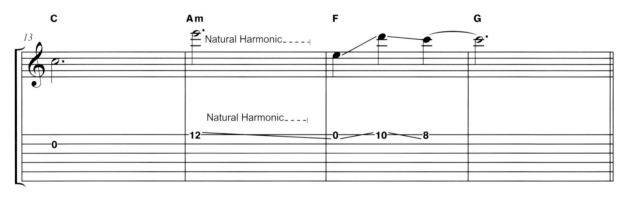

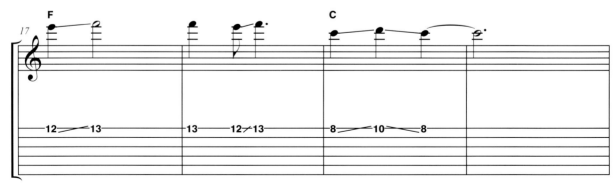

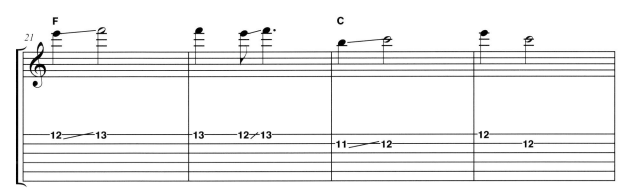

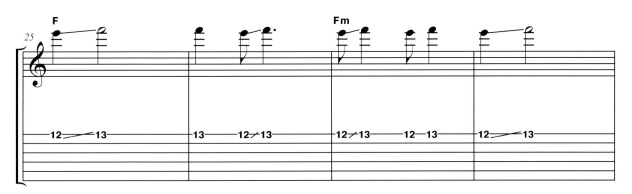

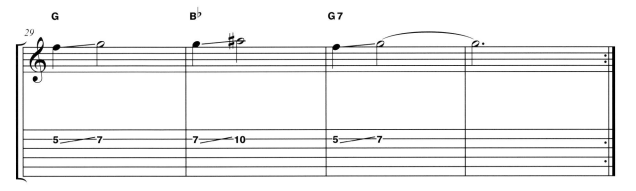

'Busted Tooth'

Here is a fun boogie to get your toes a-tappin'. I have included the rhythm just so you rhythm players don't feel left out. Seriously, this a good one to trade licks on, so find a partner and riff away. The lead part is played by pinching the notes with your pick, thus getting a squelched bell-like sound. It's a cool technique made popular by ZZ Top guitarist Billy Gibbons, who supposedly uses a coin as a pick! To achieve this squelching, turn your pick at a 90-degree angle to the string and 'dig' into the string. What you should get is similar to a harmonic but with a tougher sound. In measure 17, there are too many notes to talk about other than to say that this is one of those moments when I take advantage of the open string to play a double-picked excursion up the E string. It's really just a lunatic thing I came up with when I had drunk too much coffee.

BUSTED TOOTH (RHYTHM) CD track 48

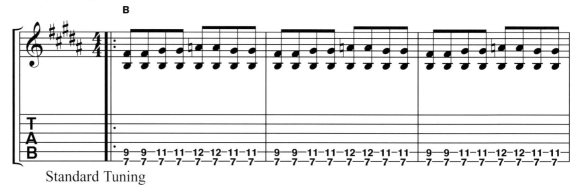

Standard Tuning

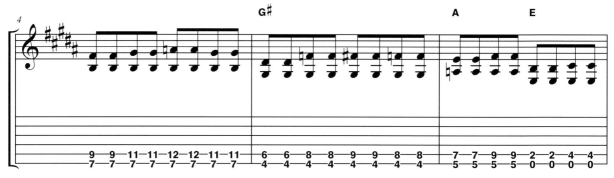

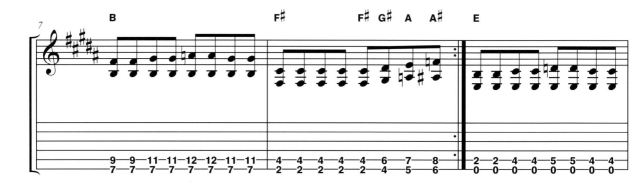

BUSTED TOOTH (LEAD) CD track 48

pinched notes throughout

continued overleaf

BUSTED TOOTH (LEAD) *continued*

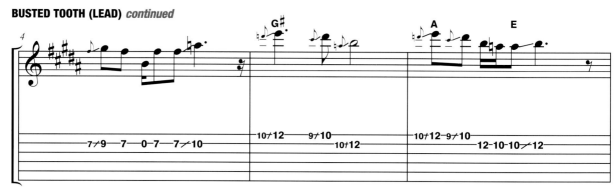

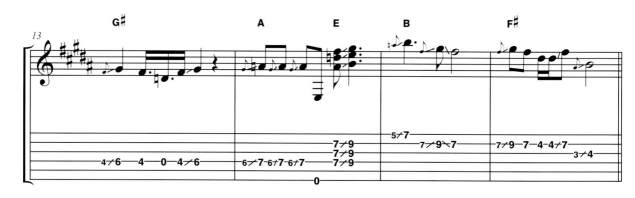

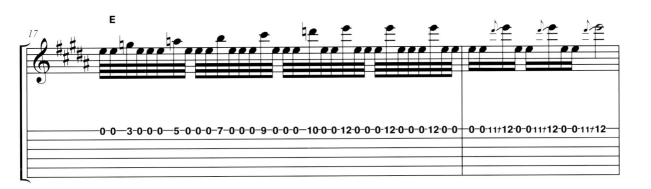

Swing

While it's not quite possible to do everything on a six-string standard-tuned guitar that one could do on a triple-neck eight-string pedal steel guitar, I have decided to include a couple of western swing styled pieces to give you the experience of trying this out. It's actually kind of fun! The two exercises in this chapter use a relatively standard 32-bar swing-era song form.

'Swing 05'

The chord changes in 'Swing 05' are borrowed from the jazz standard 'Lady Be Good,' but these chord changes and the form represent several similar tunes of the swing era. We are playing in the key of G, and as always I try to incorporate a few open third string G licks to accommodate it. The double string run in measures 9-12 is an attempt to emulate some lap or pedal steel sounds. In measure ten watch out for the slide from the 12th fret to the 15/16th; this requires that you 'slant' the slide, which isn't too difficult since that's what the slide wants to do anyways – lap and pedal steel players are constantly employing the 'slant' effect to achieve the sounds they get. Measure 15 has another 'Brozman,' that technique where you play the harmonic, then take the slide behind the nut and allow it to 'roll' over and slide through the accompanying notes.

'Speedy Country'

I based the chord changes of this one on a standard western swing I-vi-ii-V pattern. If you have never heard the guitar/pedal steel duo of Jimmy Bryant and Speedy West you owe it to yourself to go out immediately and purchase *Stratosphere Boogie*, a compilation of their best recorded instrumentals. Examining the first two bars of the slide run here you might notice that you are simply following an A major triad, a common device using single-string and double-string phrases around a central chord. In measure seven, once again, I utilize the open string (first) to get a 'quickie' phrase in over the E9 chord. Measures 13-14 have a 'falling down' effect, single-picked triplets which descend through the chord changes.

Tempo: Fast swing: 200 bpm

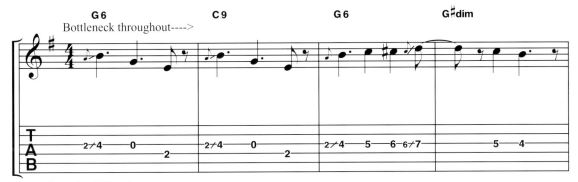

Standard Tuning

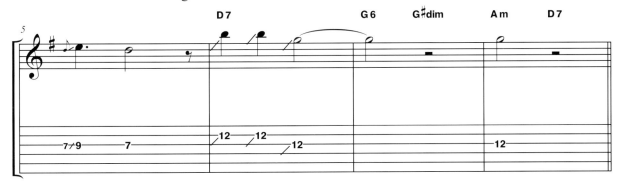

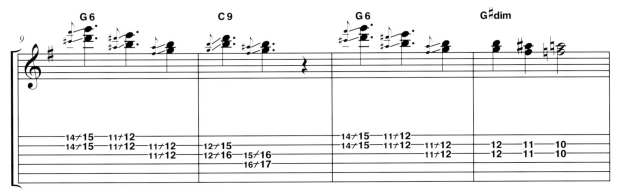

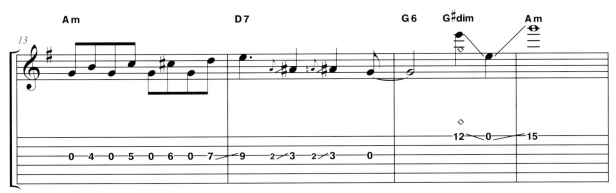

SWING 05 *continued*

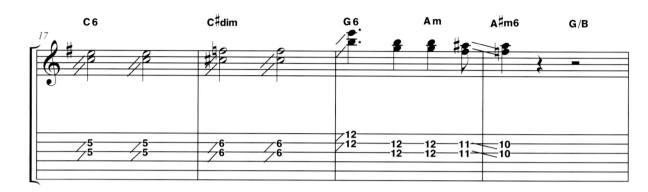

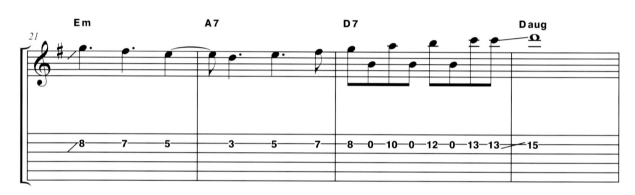

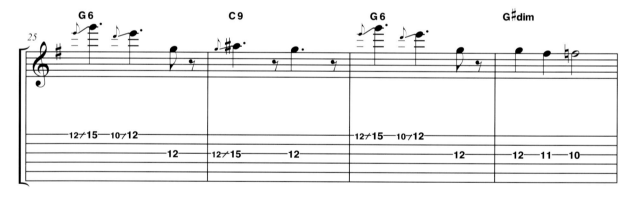

Tempo: Fast swing: 200 bpm

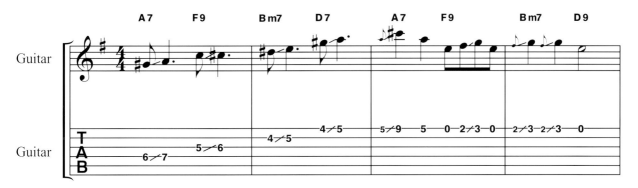

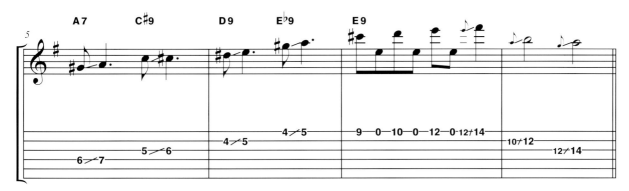

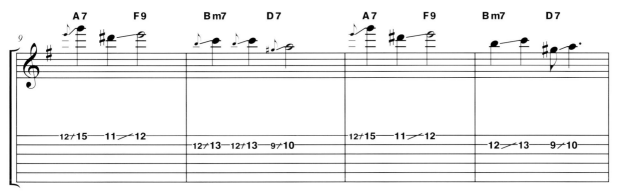

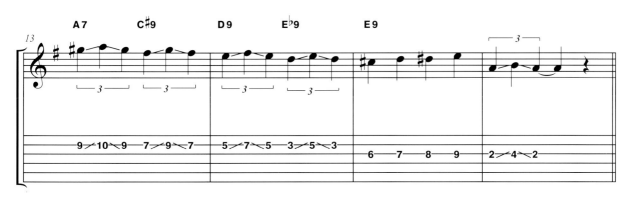

continued overleaf

SPEEDY COUNTRY *continued*

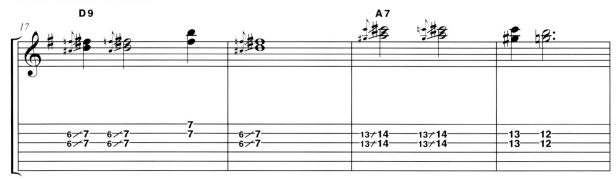

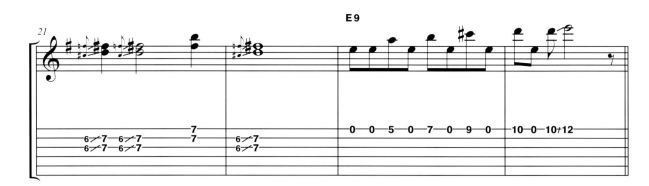

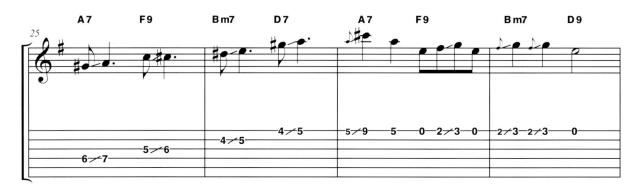

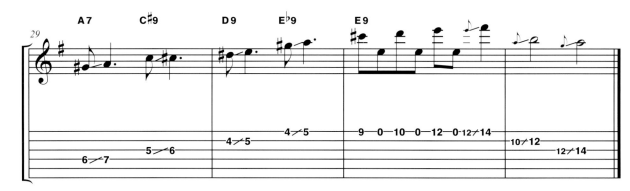

Alternate tunings and advanced fingerstyle compositions

The compositions in this chapter use a few new tunings: open C (CGCGCE), DADGAD, and D7 (DADF#CD). Though these are extended compositions, they contain very little new in terms of technique and if you are up for playing some longer pieces these should provide you with a bit of fun.

'Watermelon Seeds'

C tuning (CGCGCE) has a killer low-resonant sound. If you play in this tuning I recommend using medium gauge (13-56) strings or heavier: the drop in tension on the strings can make it difficult to get a good sound with your slide. This tune was inspired by a Leo Kottke tune called 'Watermelon,' and except for the intro it should played in robust early-Kottke fashion. An alternating bass with melody notes highlighted on the first string drive this song through the first verse (Part B). The second verse lowers the dynamic by bringing in some harmonics.

WATERMELON SEEDS CD track 51

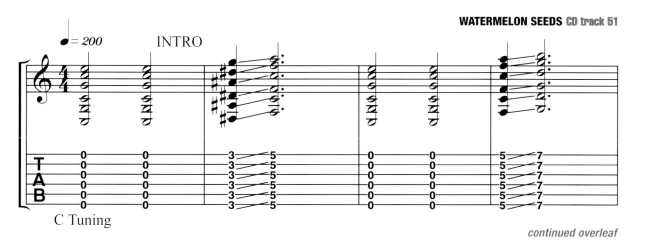

C Tuning

continued overleaf

WATERMELON SEEDS *continued*

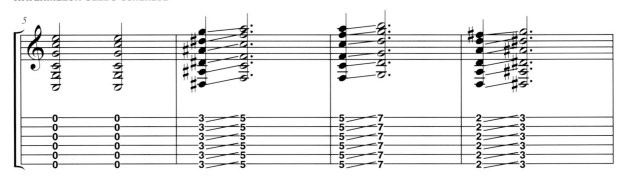

PART A

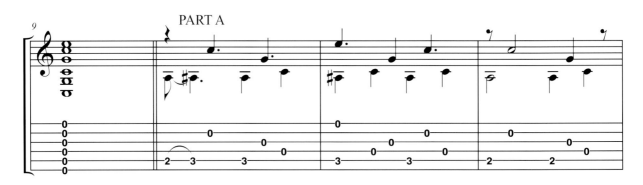

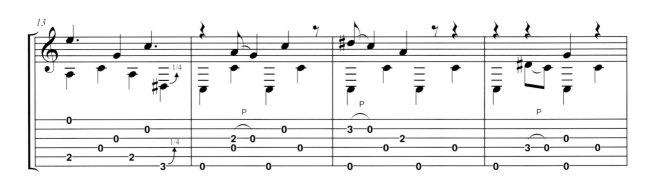

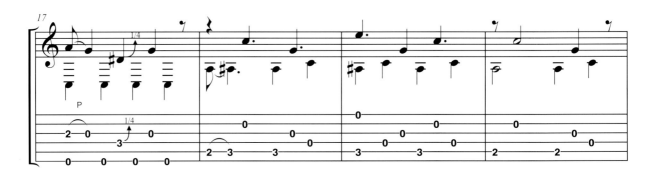

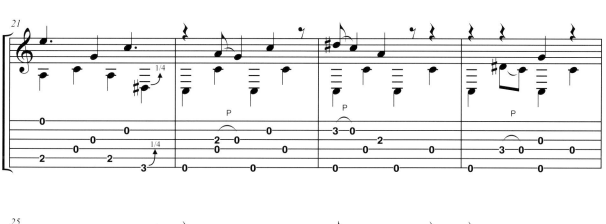

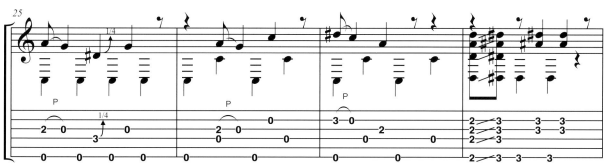

end PART A

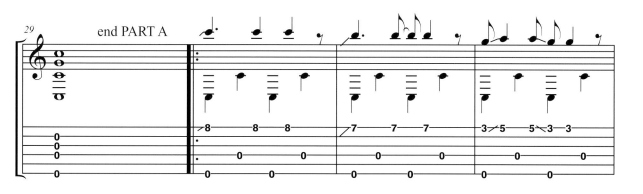

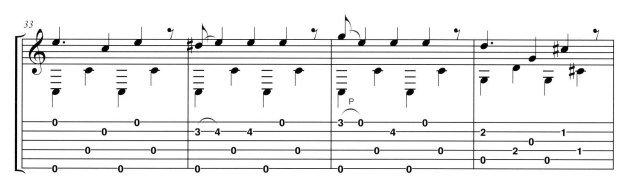

continued overleaf

WATERMELON SEEDS *continued*

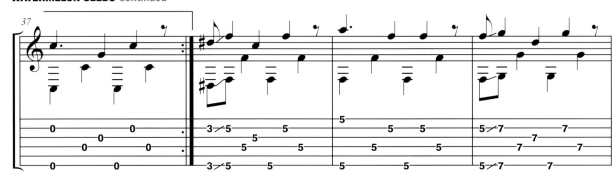

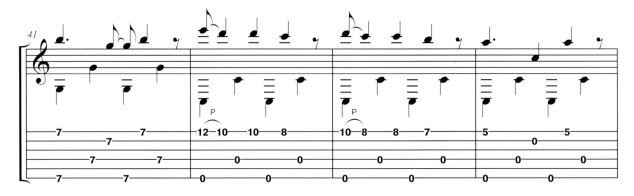

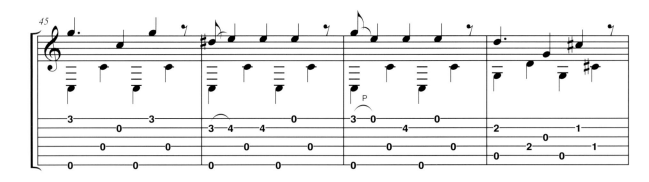

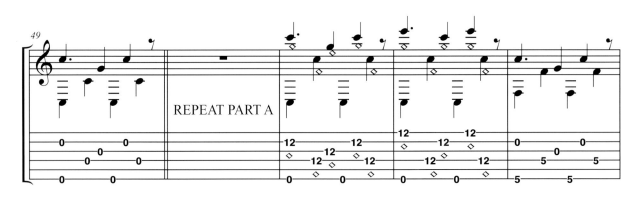

REPEAT PART A

continued overleaf

WATERMELON SEEDS *continued*

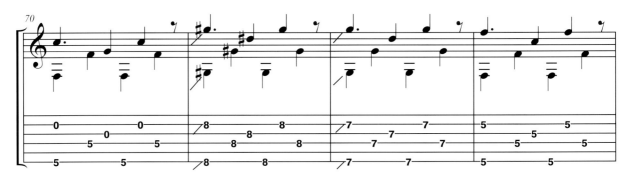

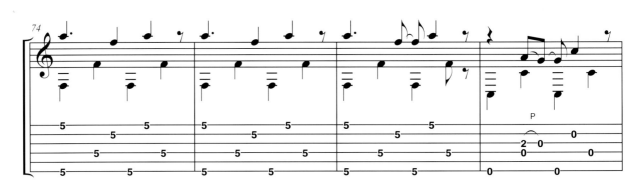

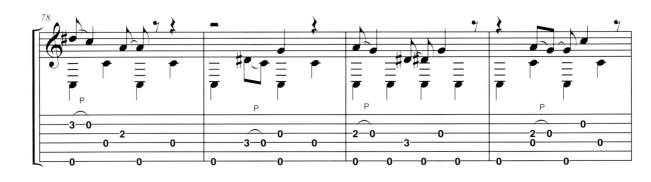

'Big Chief/Little Warrior'

Also in C tuning (CGCGCE), this composition evokes a bit of a warpath. The intro section uses a 'popping' technique, but rather than the thumb it will be the index finger that pops the notes on the fourth string – much like a funk bass player would do (think Larry Graham). The bottleneck enters the fray in measure eight. In measures 25-28 the left-hand first finger barres the third fret and the ring finger plays the low bass on the sixth string. Then on beat three the slide drops down to barre the entire fifth fret. In measures 33-36 the right hand 'grabs' the strings with four fingers, but the final beat is a downward strum with the thumb.

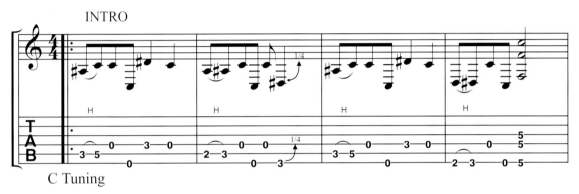

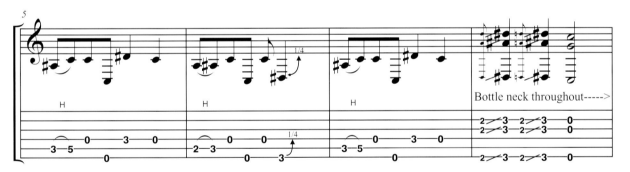

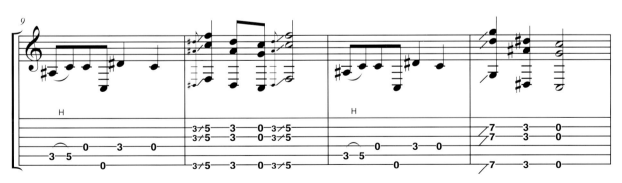

continued overleaf

BIG CHIEF/LITTLE WARRIOR *continued*

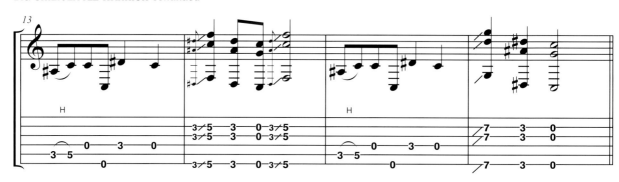

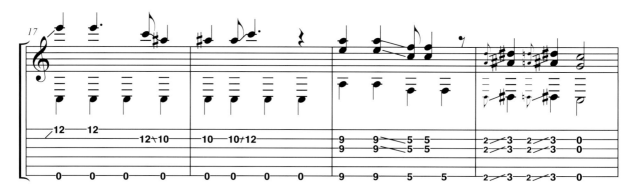

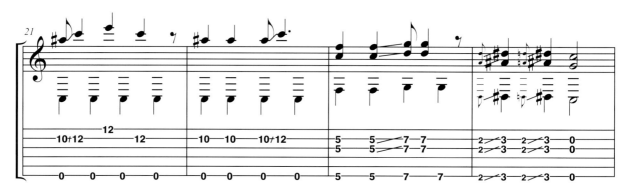

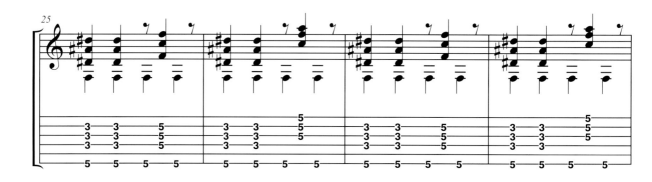

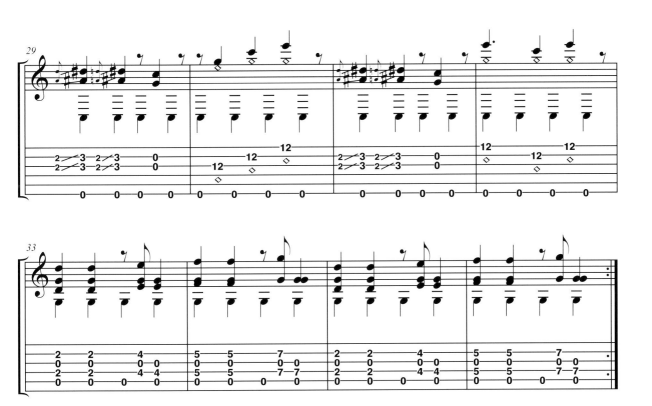

'DADGAD'

DADGAD is a tuning used by many in the modern fingerstyle arena. To get to DADGAD from open D tuning, tune your 3rd string (G) up a half-step from F# back up to G. In DADGAD you have a suspension that neither resolves to the major nor to the minor 3rd. It is a popular tuning for players performing Celtic-inspired pieces and has been used effectively by Jimmy Page, Martin Simpson, and Pierre Bensusan.

DADGAD CD track 53

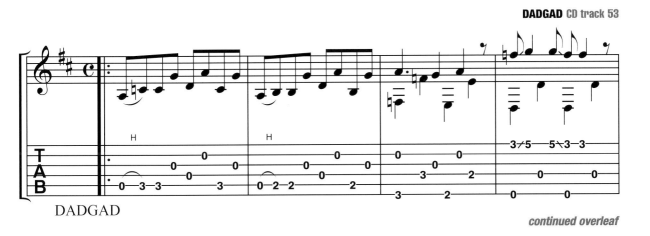

DADGAD

continued overleaf

DADGAD *continued*

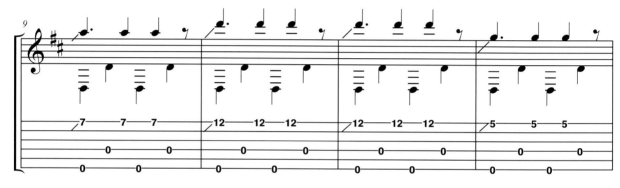

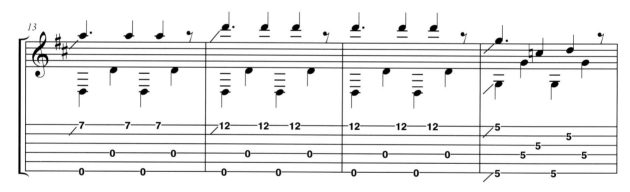

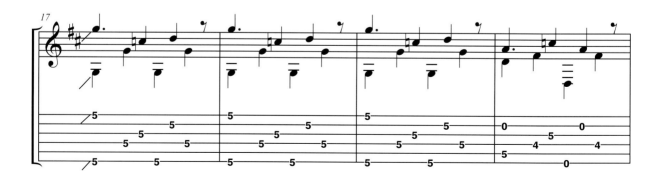

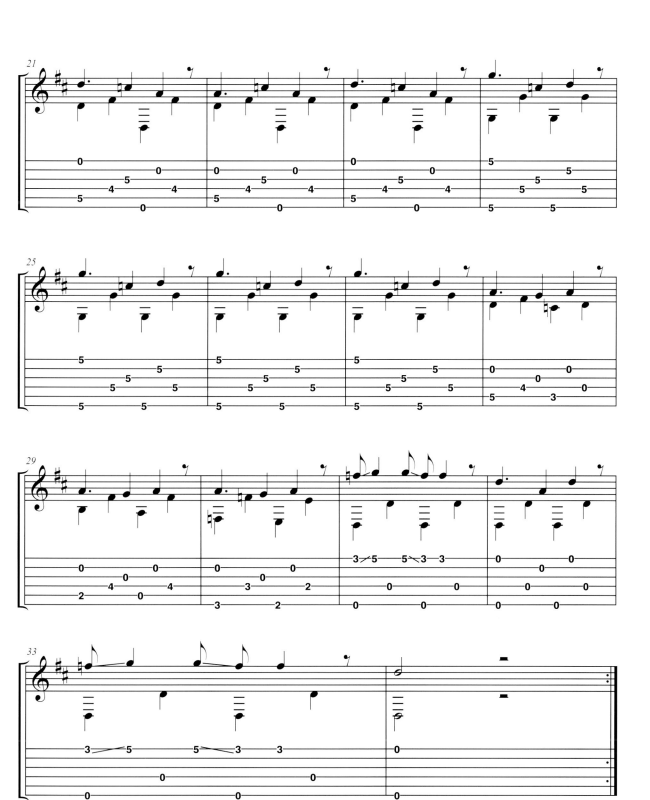

'Le Petit Nicolas'

D7 tuning (DADF#CD) is one I stumbled on when I was going between open D and open C tunings. The C note on the second string gives a mischievous quality to the sound, hence I named this composition after my two-year-old son. The intro to this song is a free-time exploration of an Arabian sounding scale. The intro lick is achieved by allowing the slide to 'bounce' on the first string, thus creating a hammer-on/pull-off effect that is quick and subtle. In measure eight we have another 'Brozman.' After playing the harmonic at the 12th fret, place the slide behind the nut, then 'roll' it over the nut and back along the string to play the remaining notes of the phrase.

In measure 11 we move to a 'second' intro, very similar in technique to Son House's octave 'pop.' Bass notes in this section (except the open string) are fretted with the index finger.

LE PETIT NICOLAS CD track 54

INTRO: Arabic sounding; free time
Tempo: 168bpm

D7 Tuning

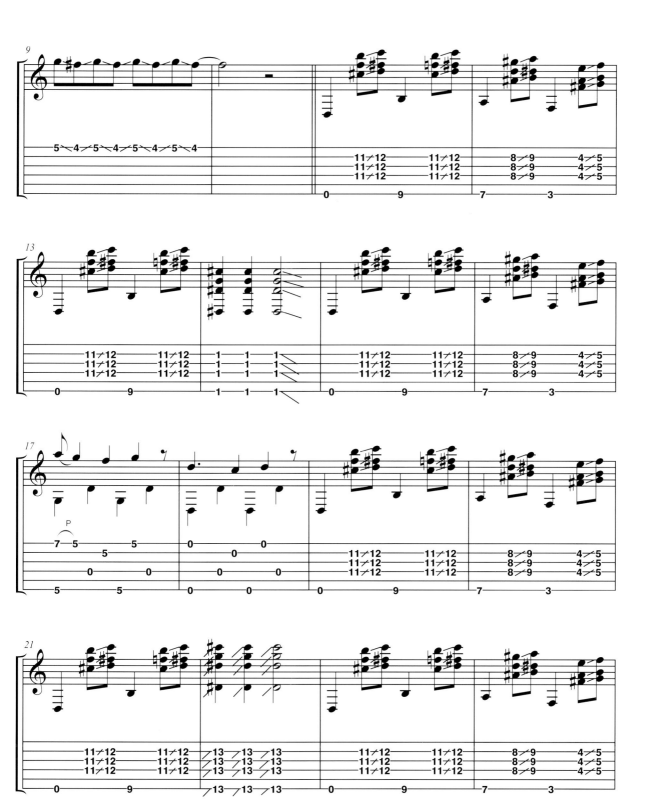

continued overleaf

LE PETIT NICOLAS *continued*

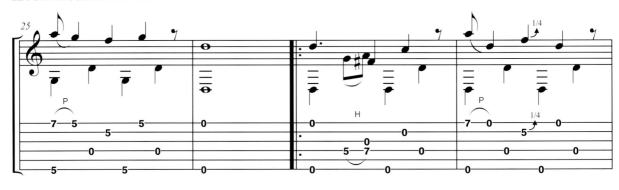

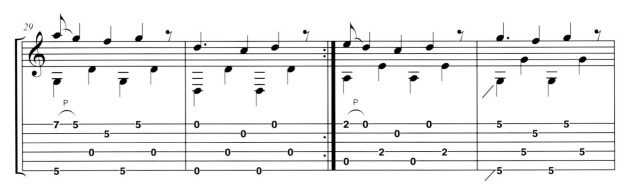

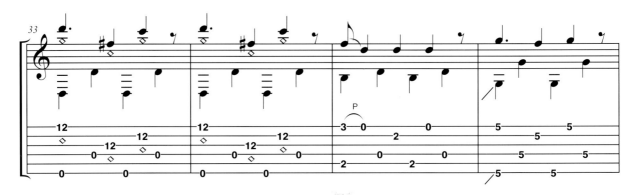

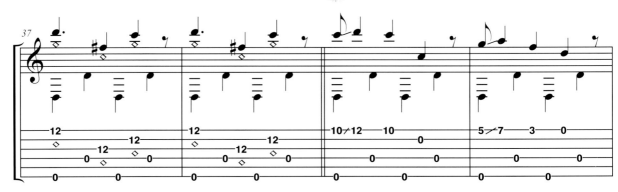

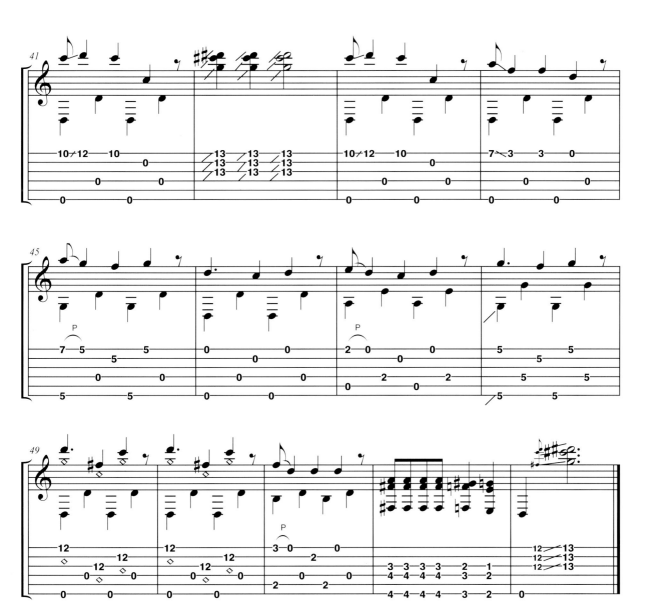

A final word on open tunings

Open tunings can evoke the creative spirit. I invite you to experiment with them and come up with your own compositions. I think part of the fun of playing in open tunings is that the chords and scales you know in standard tuning simply don't work. This can cause one of two reactions: 1) I just don't know what to play, or 2) I just don't know what to play so I think I'll make something up. (Actually, there is a third reaction: if you are Pierre Bensusan you decide to learn everything you know in the new tuning.) There are as many approaches to 'making things up' as you can come with, but if that task seems too daunting try limiting yourself to experiments like these: I think I will play melody notes on just one string and an alternating bass on two strings; or try a new tuning: everything in thirds, fifths… etc.

CD track listing

All music composed and played by Pete Madsen.

TRACK 1 EXERCISE 1

TRACK 2 EXERCISE 2

TRACK 3 EXERCISE 3

TRACK 4 EXERCISE 4

TRACK 5 EXERCISE 5

TRACK 6 EXERCISE 6

TRACK 7 EXERCISE 7

TRACK 8 EXERCISE 8

TRACK 9 EXERCISE 9

TRACK 10 EXERCISE 10

TRACK 11 EXERCISE 11

TRACK 12 EXERCISE 12

TRACK 13 EXERCISE 13

TRACK 14 EXERCISE 14

TRACK 15 EXERCISE 15

TRACK 16 EXERCISE 16

TRACK 17 EXERCISE 17

TRACK 18 EXERCISE 18

TRACK 19 EXERCISE 19

TRACK 20 EXERCISE 20

TRACK 21 EXERCISE 21

TRACK 22 EXERCISE 22

TRACK 23 EXERCISE 23

TRACK 24 EXERCISE 24

TRACK 25 EXERCISE 25

TRACK 26 EXERCISE 26

TRACK 27 EXERCISE 27

TRACK 28 EXERCISE 28

TRACK 29 EXERCISE 29

TRACK 30 EXERCISE 30

TRACK 31 EXERCISE 31

TRACK 32 EXERCISE 32

TRACK 33 EXERCISE 33

TRACK 34 'SON HOUSE GROOVE'

TRACK 35 'CROSSROADS GROOVE'

TRACK 36 'POOR MAN BLUES'

TRACK 37 'BOOGIE ON A ROLL'

TRACK 38 'TAMPA RED STYLE'

TRACK 39 'CHARLIE PATTON GROOVE'

TRACK 40 'THE FORLORN'

TRACK 41 'GOIN' DOWN TO RICHMOND'

TRACK 42 'MUDDY WATERS STYLE'

TRACK 43 'STATESBORO BROS.'

TRACK 44 'GEORGE HARRISON GROOVE'

TRACK 45 'LOWELL GEORGE GROOVE'

TRACK 46 'SONNY LANDRETH STYLE'

TRACK 47 'SLEEPWALKER'

TRACK 48 'BUSTED TOOTH'

TRACK 49 'SWING 05'

TRACK 50 'SPEEDY COUNTRY'

TRACK 51 'WATERMELON SEEDS'

TRACK 52 'BIG CHIEF/LITTLE WARRIOR'

TRACK 53 'DADGAD'

TRACK 54 'LE PETIT NICOLAS'

Recommended listening

The following list is by no means exhaustive, but it is good place to start if you want to get a grounding in slide guitar.

Hula Blues: Vintage Steel Guitar (Rounder Select)
A collection of Hawaiian-style numbers that gives you a solid sampling of such influential lap slide players as Sol Hoopii, Frank Ferera, Jim and Bob (The Genial Hawaiians), Roy Smeck and others.

Slide Guitar Classics: Blues Masters, Volume 15 (Rhino Records)
This collection covers mostly electric blues, from Elmore James's version of 'Dust My Broom' to the Allman Brothers' live version of 'Statesboro Blues' – a must! However, I find the inclusion of Ry Cooder's version of 'All Shook Up' to not be the best example of his playing. Better to go out and get his first album, entitled simply *Ry Cooder* (Warner Brothers), so you can hear his version of 'Dark Is The Night, Cold Was The Ground.' It's a classic.

Chicago Slide Guitar Masters: From Tampa Red to Elmore James (Saga Blues)
This collection, produced by a French label, is broken into two sections: pre-war and post-war. A good sampling of the Chicago scene, with contributions from Kokomo Arnold, Muddy Waters, Johnny Shines and, of course, Tampa Red and Elmore James.

Crucial Slide Guitar Blues (Alligator Records)
This collection is mainly rockin' electric blues featuring some great playing by Johnny Winter, Lil' Ed & The Blues Imperials, and Sonny Landreth.

Leo Kottke: 6 and 12 String Guitar (Takoma)
Originally put out on John Fahey's Takoma label, whose catalog is now owned by Fantasy Records. A must for anyone who loves acoustic 12-string guitar. That would be me. Some incredible right hand technique and some cool slide stuff as well.

David Lindley: El Rayo-X (Elektra)
I like this purely for Lindley's rendition of 'Mercury Blues' played on lap slide. There are some other notable selections here too, but nothing rocks quite the way that does.

Sonny Landreth: Grant Street (Sugarhill)

This live recording features Landreth's trio performing in his native New Orleans. A great sampling of an unheralded player.

Rory Gallagher: Against the Grain (Buddha/BMG)

A 1970s blues rocker who plays like he means it. Gallagher's sound is stripped down, raw and energetic. 'Souped Up Ford' has an amped slide sound that puts the pedal to the metal.

Kelly Joe Phelps: Shine Eyed Mister Zen (Rykodisc)

Kelly Joe Phelps has a unique playing style: he plays lap-style slide on a normal old Dreadnought guitar that has been modified for slide playing. He also plays in open D tuning, which is a tuning that isn't used much by lap-style players. Check out 'The House Carpenter' on this recording; it's some of the best acoustic slide playing that you will ever hear.

Bob Brozman: Devil's Slide (Rounder Select)

Brozman is today's master of acoustic slide guitar. Playing mostly on National resonator guitars, he conjures up old blues, swing era, calypso and any other influences he can get his hands on for this recording. It's fast paced, kinda crazy and a hell of a lot of fun.

Old blues recordings

Many people don't want to bother with old blues recordings because the sound quality can be particularly poor. Don't be put off by this; hearing the original blues recordings can be an invigorating experience. Yazoo puts out some of the better mastered CDs. Advances in technology has lead to the elimination of a lot of the 'scratchiness' heard in early recordings. I have also run across some amazing deals in old blues box sets. Acoustic Music Records – out of Germany – has put together a 4 CD collection called *The Essential Country Blues Guitar Collection* which has the cream of the crop of acoustic blues guitar from the 1920 to the 1940s. Of course, not all of it is slide, but there are many choice cuts from Charlie Patton, Robert Johnson, Blind Willie Johnson and many others – and the liner notes tell you what tuning the player is using on each track!

Index

Acknowledgements

I would to thank the following people for their help with this book. Everybody at *Acoustic Guitar* magazine, including: Teja Gerken, Scott Nygard, Nicole Solis, and Andrew DuBrock (thanks for the Finale help!). My students, who let me try out some of these exercises on them – "No, like this!" Ben Bonham, who is a wonderful slide player and, I hear, a mean windsurfer. Bob Brozman, who opened doors to the possibilities of slide playing for me. Moonshine Slides, who make Mudslides – my favorites! National Guitar Company, for STILL making resonator guitars the way they used to. John Morrish, for his fine and timely editing. And, lastly, thanks to all the players who have used a piece of bone, glass, ceramic, steel, brass or whatever on steel strings to create some of the finest music on the planet.